Arthur Penrhyn Stanley

The Athanasian Creed

with a preface on the general recommendations of the Ritual commission

Arthur Penrhyn Stanley

The Athanasian Creed
with a preface on the general recommendations of the Ritual commission

ISBN/EAN: 9783337313272

Printed in Europe, USA, Canada, Australia, Japan

Cover: Foto ©Andreas Hilbeck / pixelio.de

More available books at **www.hansebooks.com**

THE ATHANASIAN CREED

*WITH A PREFACE ON
THE GENERAL RECOMMENDATIONS OF
THE RITUAL COMMISSION*

BY

ARTHUR PENRHYN STANLEY, D.D.

DEAN OF WESTMINSTER

London
MACMILLAN AND CO.
1871

All rights reserved

LONDON: PRINTED BY
SPOTTISWOODE AND CO., NEW-STREET SQUARE
AND PARLIAMENT STREET

(Republished from the Contemporary Review)

PREFACE.

THE FOLLOWING PAGES[1] relate to the present obligation to recite the Athanasian Creed in the public services, which in parish churches devolves partly on the clergyman, partly on the laity; in cathedral and collegiate churches usually on the laity. Within the last year this use has been all but unanimously[2] condemned by a Royal Commission appointed (amongst other objects) for the purpose of considering this question; as was expressed in strong terms by the Minister (the late Lord Derby) under whose auspices the appointment was made.

It is not chiefly with a view of urging the omission or change of this Rubric that these pages are republished. It is rather with the view of showing that such a relaxation, which in some form has become inevitable, ought to give

[1] Published (in substance) in the *Contemporary Review* of August and November 1870.
[2] See pp. 73-92.

offence to no reasonable or religious mind, and that in fact it has virtually received the adhesion of the representatives of all parties and schools in the Church. For this purpose of pacification and of conciliation, it has seemed to me that a brief history and description of the Athanasian Creed, and of its treatment by the Royal Commission, might not be unacceptable.

But I am unwilling, as one of that body, that it should be thought that this change, salutary and indispensable though it be, and sanctioned by the highest ecclesiastical authorities, is yet the most urgent in the recommendations of the Commission.

If the Athanasian Creed ceases to be generally read, the chief result would be felt in the relief of the many whose devotions are at present disturbed by its uncongenial notes. But there are other changes, less striking perhaps, but which would be more fruitful of consequences, for which the public opinion of the Church still more loudly calls, and of which the principles, if not the details, are sanctioned in the several Reports of the Commissioners.

Let me indicate some of these, both on account of their intrinsic concern, and also because of the incidental interest attaching to the mode in which they were treated. Three other members of the Commission have already endeavoured to clear away some misapprehensions on this subject, and I shall, therefore, be excused if I endeavour to follow in the same path.

(1) Of all the subjects which the Commission had to discuss, the least important was that which some persons suppose to have been the only cause of its appointment, viz. the vexed interpretation of the obscure Rubric on 'the 'Ornaments of the Church and the Minister.' Not only have most of the questions therein involved been settled by the Courts of Law, but the public have generally acquiesced in their almost entire insignificance. The sense of that insignificance[1] is best expressed either by the total omission of any regulation on the subject (as in the Prayer-book of the Church of Ireland and in the Directory of the Church of Scotland), or by leaving it (as in the second and fourth Reports of the Commission) without alteration as a relic of antiquity.

(2) The New Table of Lessons, which was, in

[1] See Second Report, p. iv. (Remarks of the Solicitor-General and of the Dean of Westminster).

the judgment of many, esteemed an almost impossible undertaking, was unanimously adopted, both by the Committee appointed to make the selection, and by the whole body of the Commissioners. This unanimity was remarkable, as showing how the most diverse elements embraced by the most comprehensive of Christian Churches could be brought to an absolute agreement when they approached a question where party spirit was not involved, and where they were drawn upwards to the sacred and primitive sources above the region from which the streams of modern controversy divide. It was a natural prelude to the concord, on a still larger scale, of the scholars who have been appointed to assist in the revision of the text itself of the English Bible.

A like unanimity prevailed in regard to the occasional substitution of other Psalms for those appointed in the Psalter. Any measure including the revision of the Lectionary would be manifestly incomplete without this indispensable addition.

(3) The principle of rendering the services more flexible had already been sanctioned, in numberless instances, by popular use. The

Commissioners were but called to legalise variations from a rigid rule of uniformity alike contrary to common sense and religious devotion. In the week-day services, as in the services for the Communion, for the Visitation of the Sick, and for the Burial of the Dead, the freedom which all other Churches have accorded, and which many members of our own take for themselves, are recommended, if not with absolute unanimity, yet with sufficient agreement to show that there could be no serious objection raised against it.

(4) To those who study the Minutes it will appear that there was, and is, no adequate reason why the same principle should not be applied to the Sunday services, to the Marriage service, to the Commination service, to the Confirmation service, and to the Baptismal service. In all these cases the same liberty that has been granted in the other services is already freely taken both by Bishops and clergy; and, in most of those cases, at one period of the sessions of the Commission, some latitude was intended to have been recommended. In one case especially, the Baptismal service, the removal of what is confessedly one of the chief

stumbling-blocks in parochial Churches—the requirement of the sponsorial system from those who can neither understand nor discharge its duties—was actually carried at the generous instigation of one of the Commissioners,[1] whose usual predilections were an ample guarantee for its pacific reception by the High Church school; and it is lamentable to think that it was afterwards lost through the adverse circumstances which marred the successful conclusion of so large a part of the labours of the Commissioners.

(5) This is the place to notice (what amply appears from the Minutes) how greatly the character of the Commission was altered in the course of the three years of its sessions. Not to speak of the necessary changes through the death or withdrawal of its members—the fact is well known that during the last five months of its existence several important Commissioners (including the Primate), whose influence was well known to have been in favour of relaxing the bonds which fettered the usefulness of the Church, were kept away by illness or other causes at critical moments of decision. But,

[1] Fourth Report, p. 113.

though their absence affected the technical conclusions at which in some cases the Commission arrived, this miscarriage has been sufficiently rectified by the detailed expression of their opinions as soon as they had the opportunity of utterance; and this, whilst it explains the somewhat anomalous state in which the Final Report is presented, furnishes the public with a true index as to the practical conclusions of the actual majority.

(6) It was the hope entertained, by some at least, that when the Royal Commissioners commenced their sittings in the Jerusalem Chamber the results would have been worthy of those eminent men who had in 1689 occupied the same apartment, under the guidance of Tillotson and Burnet, for a similar object. If this hope has been in part disappointed, in part it has been more than gratified. Whatever may be the actual effect of the Royal Commission of 1867, it will have at least proved that the leaders of the several schools of ecclesiastical thought could combine for the promotion of measures for the true interests of the Church. It will have shown that there is a determination to adapt the services of the Prayer-book to the altered

state of England without destroying its comprehensive character or its elevated language. It will have shown that the Revision of 1662, with all the miserable distractions which it left behind, was not final. It will have shown that the rule which was called by a pious Churchman of the last generation the only Rubric of the Gospels,[1] has received due attention. It will have shown that the charitable and large construction put on the formularies of the Church by its best members has been and must be openly recognised. It will have shown that, but for the accidental circumstances above indicated, the principles which the Commissioners have sanctioned in a large number of cases would have been successfully applied throughout the Prayer-book.

If these results are accomplished, and bear their natural fruits, the labours of the Commission will not have been in vain; and the Church of England will be strengthened to meet whatever trials may be in store for it, not by idle forebodings of evils which may never come, but by clearing away the imperfections which mar its grace and clog its

[1] 'Use not vain repetitions.'

usefulness. It is not for any individual to dictate or suggest the mode in which these changes should be carried out. But I may be pardoned for expressing the hope that they will be effected, as like changes have in former times been effected, by the necessary alteration of the Law. No doubt the Law, as expressed in the Rubrics of the Prayer-book, never has been, perhaps never can be, carried out literally in every particular, under all circumstances, and in all places. This has been sufficiently shown for past times by the excellent work of Canon Robertson entitled, with as much humour as truth, 'How shall we 'conform to the Liturgy?' And, should the requisite liberty not be conceded by an authorised relaxation of the existing enactments, the clergy and congregations of the Church of England will not be exceeding the freedom established by former precedents if they adopt for themselves the changes urged by such high authority as that involved in the recommendations of the Royal Commission. But unquestionably it would be far better that the improvements which the Church and country require should be effected by the only process which can place them on an equality with the inconvenient usages to be superseded by them.[1] It is hard on those who wish to obey the law to be placed at a disadvantage with those who have no scruple in setting the law at defiance. This is an occasion, such as may not soon recur, for the nation to assert its right of guiding its own religious worship. Nonconformists have as clear a right, as obvious an interest, in promoting the amelioration of a great national institution as they had in the ecclesiastical legislation of 1559, 1641, and 1662. Churchmen have a stronger ground than ever for adapting the Prayer-book to the needs of the time, and for rendering its services as widely available as possible. Whatever objections may be brought in detail against the recommendations of the Commissioners, and however much its proceedings suffered from accidental hindrances, the principles which it affirms are obvious, and will be a guide to legislation such as no Parliament need refuse to follow.

[1] I do not here enter on the question whether the necessary changes might not be effected by an enactment giving increased power to the existing Ordinary, or to some analogous authority.

DEANERY, WESTMINSTER:
February 4, 1871.

CONTENTS.

ATHANASIAN CREED.

                                          PAGE

I. ITS AUTHORSHIP 1–6
    Its general reception founded on the belief that it
        was by Athanasius 2
    This belief mistaken 5

II. ITS INTERNAL CHARACTERISTICS . . . 7
    1. Its rhythmical form 7
        Advantages 8
        Disadvantages 10
    2. Its clearness 12
        Absence of mystery 13
        The word 'incomprehensible' . . . 14
    3. Its obscurity 14
        Ambiguities of the word 'substance' . . 15
            „   „   'person' . . 16
        Hypostasis—identical with *substance*, afterwards
            opposed to it 17–21
        Persona—change of meaning . . . 21
        Person—change of meaning . . . 22
        General confusion 24

	PAGE
4. The Damnatory Clauses	26
History of the older anathemas	26
Peculiarity of the damnatory clauses	27
Their meaning	29
Scruples concerning them	32

III. PECULIARITIES OF ITS USE IN THE CHURCH OF ENGLAND 35

1. Public recital confined to the Church of England . 35
   Rejected by the American Episcopal Church . 36
2. Faulty translation 37
3. Long desuetude 39
4. Condemnation of the Eastern Churches, incompatible with Anglican sympathy . . . 42

IV. ITS ADVANTAGES 50

1. Its historical curiosity 50
2. Its latitude in regard to modern controversy . 51

ITS DISADVANTAGES 51

Especially—

1. Exaltation of correct belief into the first of virtues 52
   Irrelevancy of Mark xvi. 16 . . . 53
2. Encouragement of party and personal animosities against individuals 55
   Occasional applications 57

V. INTERPRETATIONS 59

Parallel case of Solemn League and Covenant . 61
Also of the Three Political Services . . 67

CONTENTS. xvii

                                                                                  PAGE

VI. JUDGMENT OF THE RITUAL COMMISSION .

    Condemnation of the Damnatory Clauses by the Explanatory Note of seven Commissioners . 73

    Condemnation of the enforced use of the Creed by nineteen Commissioners 74

1. Archbishop of Canterbury 75
2. Earl Stanhope 76
3. Lord Portman 77
4. The Earl of Harrowby 77
5. The Bishop of Winchester 77
6. The Bishop of St. David's 78
7. Lord Ebury 79
8. Mr. John Abel Smith, M.P. . . . 79
9. The Bishop of Carlisle 79
10. The Right Hon. Spencer H. Walpole . . 80
11. The Right Hon. Sir Joseph Napier . . 80
12. Sir Travers Twiss, the Queen's Advocate . . 80
13. Mr. Charles Buxton, M.P. 81
14. The Dean of Westminster 83
15. The Dean of Lincoln (Regius Professor of Divinity at Cambridge) 87
16. The Rev. Canon Payne Smith (Regius Professor of Divinity at Oxford) 88
17. The Rev. Henry Venn 90
18. The Rev. W. G. Humphry (Vicar of St. Martin's-in-the-Fields) 90
19. The Rev. T. W. Perry 91

	PAGE
Summary of the judgment	92
Explanatory Note—Parallel explanations of the dogma of the Pope's Infallibility	94
VII. CONCLUSION	104

THE
ATHANASIAN CREED.

THERE are certain documents in ecclesiastical literature which have a living history of their own, interesting and instructive, even irrespectively of their contents. One such is the celebrated confession variously known as the Hymn *Quicunque Vult*, the 'Confession of the Catholic Faith,' or 'the Creed of 'St. Athanasius.' It has now reached, as regards the Church of England, what must be considered by all as a critical moment in its existence. It has been the subject of innumerable letters of attack and defence in public journals. It has been discussed in a Commission appointed by the Crown for considering the Rubrics of the Church. It has been the subject of elaborate criticism and suggestion, as well from those who admire it, as from those who depreciate it.

Under these circumstances a short review of its main characteristics may be desirable.

I. Its first reception and actual use in Christendom is one of the most remarkable instances of the lasting effect of those literary mistakes [1] which have exercised so great an influence over the history of the Church. It is to be classed in this respect with the works of Dionysius the Areopagite, which formed the basis of the popular notions of the Celestial Hierarchy; with the false Decretals of the early Popes and early Emperors, which formed the basis of the Pontifical power. Under the shadow of a great name it crept, like those other documents, into general acceptance; and then, when that shadow was exorcised by the spell of critical enquiry, still retained the place which it had won under false pretences. Through the Middle Ages it was always quoted as the work of Athanasius. In the sixteenth century a title derived from the champion of Christian orthodoxy still dazzled the vision of the Reformers. In the Augsburg Confession, and in the Thirty-nine Articles, in the Belgic and in the Bohemian Confessions, in the 'Ecclesiastical Polity' of Hooker, it is unhesitatingly received as the 'Creed of St. Athana-'sius.' No one at that time entertained any doubt of its authorship. The very year of its composition was fixed; the very hole in the Abbey of St. Maximin, near the Black Gate at Treves, was pointed out as the spot where Athanasius had written it in the concealment of his western exile. Yet it is now known

[1] There is no reason to suppose that the assumption of the name of Athanasius was in the first instance a deliberate forgery, in the vulgar sense of the word. But it already bore its present title in the eighth century; and the inference that he was the author was natural, and from the ninth century spread rapidly.

with absolute certainty not only that Athanasius never did write it, but never could have written it. The language in which it is composed was probably unknown to him. We shall see, as we proceed, that the terminology which it employs was condemned by him. It contains at least one doctrine which he would have repudiated. But just as some of the writings of Pelagius have been preserved in consequence of their having been confounded with the writings of his great adversary, St. Jerome, so the treatise of the unknown author who composed this, in some important respects, anti-Athanasian Creed, has been embalmed for posterity by its early ascription to the Father of orthodoxy. The memory of that mighty champion of the faith whose romantic adventures, as has been often remarked, make even the cold pages of Gibbon to glow, the fame of whose incantations still lingers in the Dragon of St. George, and in the Beelzebub of the mummers of the northern peasantry, has achieved this yet more important triumph. By the magic of his name this confession, of unknown origin and ambiguous character, found its way into the Western Church, and has been kept alive and retained a charmed existence even after its real character had been discovered. This curious tale has a double moral. On the one hand, it shows the marvellous power which the mere name of a great man can exercise long after the contests in which he was engaged are dead and buried—long after the church, of which he was the head and chief ornament, has been separated from the Churches which make it their boast to claim his work as their own. On the other hand, this circumstance may reconcile its stanchest adherents more easily to dealing freely with it; for, as it is evident that but for the belief in its Athanasian origin, it would never have been accepted either by the Roman or by the English Church, so now that its un-Athanasian origin is proved, the special ground of its acceptance ceases. It was urged by Burnet in 1689, and has been often urged since, that the introduction of the Athanasian Creed into the public services of the Church was in direct contravention of the decrees of the Councils of Ephesus and Chalcedon, which forbade, under severe penalties, the composition or publication of any other Creed than the Nicene. So long as the Athanasian Creed was believed to be by Athanasius himself, it might possibly have been supposed that, having been written before those decrees, it escaped their condemnation. Even thus it is impossible to plead an exemption for it which the Councils themselves do not acknowledge, and if its authorship is brought as late as the close of the fifth century, then to those who attach any importance to the decrees of General Councils, the argument of Burnet is unanswerable. But even without regard to the prohibitions of Ephesus and Chalcedon, the removal of the prestige of Athanasius's name throws us back entirely on its internal value.

A book may be anonymous and yet be true, sacred, even inspired. But then the proofs of its truth and inspiration must be very strong. An institution may have been founded on error, and yet be worth preserving for its general beneficence. But that beneficence must then be its sole recommendation. The history of the reception of the Creed of St. Athanasius is like the parallel history of the reception of the Pope's Infallibility—'gangrened with imposture;' not wilful imposture it may be, not conscious fraud, but still leaving it so destitute of historical foundation as to render doubly imperative the duty of testing its claims to authority by its own intrinsic merits.

Before we proceed to these a few words must be spent on its probable date and authorship. The doubt of its Athanasian origin was first expressed by Gerard Voss in 1642, in his work on 'The Three 'Creeds,' and from this it spread with such rapidity, that in 1647 Jeremy Taylor adopted it in his ' Liberty 'of Prophesying;' and in 1662 the Revisers of the Prayer-book went out of their way to inject into the Rubrics[1] an expression of dissatisfaction which they did not venture to insert in the Articles. From that time scholars, whilst unanimous in disavowing its

[1] To the words, 'this confession of our Christian faith,' they added, '*commonly* called The Creed of St. Athanasius.' For the development of this, as well as of much else relating to the history of the Creed, the reader is referred to a very able and learned article in *Macmillan's Magazine* for November 1867, by ' Presbyter Academicus.' In many points this essay merely summarises the results of his arguments.

Athanasian authorship, have been engaged in the hitherto fruitless search after its unknown composer. Quesnel conjectured that it was the work of the African Bishop Vigilius, of Thapsus, A.D. 484, chiefly from the unfortunate reputation which he acquired for passing off his own works under fictitious names. Waterland, led by the apparent absence of allusion to Nestorius, and yet distinct reference to Apollinarius, and also thinking that it was founded[1] on Augustine's treatise on the Trinity, ascribed it to Hilary of Arles, A D. 429.[2] Mr. Harvey, believing that it was written prior to Augustine's treatise, and judging, not unwarrantably, from its denunciation of everything approaching to Apollinarianism, that it was composed by some one who was accused of that heresy, and took this ungenerous mode of expurgation (to which we shall hereafter recur), refers it to Victricius, Bishop of Rouen, A.D. 401, and thinks that the title 'Athanasian' came by mistake from the name of Anastasius, the Pope before whom Victricius defended himself. A grave question

---

[1] That it was not founded simply or exclusively on St. Augustine's *Treatise on the Trinity*, may be concluded from the following reasons:—
1. There is in that treatise (as will be noticed hereafter) but a very slight approach to the damnatory clauses.
2. The arguments on the Incarnation are differently put.
3. The bulk of the treatise abounds in speculations about mystical numbers, and metaphysical analyses of human nature, of which there is no trace in the Creed.

[2] It is much to be lamented that as late as this year (1871) a new edition of Waterland's *Treatise* has been put forth without the slightest reference to the arguments of Mr. Harvey, Mr. Ffoulkes, or Mr. Swainson.

has recently been started by Mr. Ffoulkes, whether, in the absence of any certain indications of an earlier date, it is not of the time of Charlemagne. It is then that we have the first positive proof of its appearance in any manuscript authorities, and unquestionably it bears a striking resemblance to the style of the theological expositions put forth by that energetic Prince. 'This is the Catholic Faith,' says Charlemagne, in his own paraphrase of the Apostles' Creed, 'which every 'one keeping whole and undefiled shall have ever-'lasting life.'

II. We now pass to its internal characteristics. There are four points, all of singular interest, both in themselves and in the subsequent developments through which they have passed.

1. Its form (as is implied in what was probably its original title) is not like that of the other creeds, a series of historical or dogmatical statements, but a metrical arrangement of propositions artificially and elaborately strung together. It was a prose treatise composed in the rhythm of the *Te Deum*. It was not only 'the Confession of the Catholic faith,' but 'the 'Psalm *Quicunque Vult*.' It was never regarded as one of 'the Three *Creeds*' either by the ancient Church or the modern Roman Church.[1] Every sentence is a verse, and the whole is a triumphant pæan. It is this which contains the secret (morally speaking) of its

Its rhythmical form.

---

[1] Swainson *On Athanasian Creed*, pp. 11-16.

Advantages of this form.

chief attractions, and (dogmatically speaking) of some of its chief defects. On the one hand, it is thus connected with a good side even of the ancient creeds properly so called—namely, their poetic character as thankful expressions of gratitude for the mercies of God to man. It may be worth while to quote a striking passage from Arnold's Sermons, in which this is well set forth with regard to their public use :—

In the Catechism, the Apostles' Creed, as we all know, is made a sort of text for instruction in Christian truth ; in the Baptismal Service, and in that for the Sick, it is made a touchstone, to know whether a man is fit to enter, or whether he may be considered as remaining to the end in, the society of Christians. But in our daily service it partakes much more of the nature of a triumphant hymn ; and accordingly, not only is it left to the choice of the congregation whether it shall be said or sung, but it might be imagined that the Church esteemed the latter the preferable method : for whereas the Rubric directs that·the psalms and other hymns shall be either *said or sung*, of the Creeds it is directed, in a contrary order, that they shall be either *sung or said.* This, indeed, may only be accident, though, if it be, it is a curious coincidence ; but whether it be accident or design, it certainly affords a very good illustration of the light in which the Creeds should be regarded ; not as reviving the memory of old disputes, and a sort of declaration of war against those who may not agree with us in them, but as principally a free and triumphant confession of thanksgiving to God for all the mighty works which He has done for us.

In accordance with this feeling, the famous theologian whose words have just been cited, at a time when it was unusual even in larger churches, had the Nicene Creed sung, not said, in Rugby Chapel.[1] It is due to this peculiarity that many of the objections to the Athanasian Creed, which occur when we hear it baldly recited, as in our parish churches, are softened as we hear it chanted in our great cathedrals. The grand crash of music drowns the dissonance of the jarring words, and the burning vehemence, the antithetical swing of the sentences is carried along on the wings of choir and organ till the sense of their particular meaning is lost in the spirit and energy of their sound. If (according to Waterland's conjecture of the time of its reception) it first started into general acceptance with the triumph of Clovis over the Arian Visigoths, or, according to another, of Charlemagne over the Byzantine power, it may in this aspect be regarded as the war-song[2] of the orthodox King or Emperor, the hymn of victory over the defeated heretics. Wherever it is still read or sung, this is probably the best aspect under which it can be considered—as a theological Song of Deborah, rejoicing over the fall of the enemies, as it was once thought, of God and of the Franks, as Deborah and Jael rejoiced over the fall of the enemies of God and of Israel. But there is another side to this poetical aspect of the Creed. If it, indeed, be a hymn, and if

[1] Except (it is instructive to add, both as an instance of his own humility and as an illustration of the contrast between the characters of the two distinguished men,) when his friend Archbishop Whately, who regarded it simply as a logical form, was present.
[2] Compare Dr. Newman's *Grammar of Assent*, p. 129.

Disadvantages of this form. its expressions are martial effusions of victorious gratitude, then in that exact proportion its dogmatic and polemic value ceases. As Arnold well observed in that same sermon:—

It seems, then, that that minute dwelling upon every word of the Creeds, which has been the practice of expositors; that careful recording what particular sect or opinion every clause may be considered as combating, so far from being necessary, in order to our using the Creeds aright in our daily service, would actually injure our use of them, by mixing up other thoughts and feelings by no means akin to those of devotion.

We cannot, to use a homely proverb, both have our cake and eat it. Poetry, no doubt, is a noble vehicle of truth; hymns are among the purest expressions of religious feeling. But poetry is, of itself, no more theology than it is science. Hymns, in proportion as they are polemical, cease to be hymns. The antithetical, rhythmical flow of the Athanasian Creed, so far as it goes, is an injury to the exact prosaic statement of the truth which it is intended to convey. Words are introduced, phrases are set in opposition to each other, for the sake of the antithesis; just as in some poems the sense is sacrificed to the metre or the rhyme. Thus, the constant opposition between 'Three' and 'One' which is evidently suggested by the necessity of the counterbalancing clauses, has no parallel in the Apostles' or Nicene Creed, or in any part of Scripture,[1] and turns on the ambiguity in which the two

[1] The only exception is the confessedly spurious verse of 1 John v. 7;

words are used in the two parts of the clause. It is this which not unnaturally produces the impression of an apparent wrangle and contradiction in the alternate repetition of the opposing sentences.[1] So again it is hardly conceivable that the verses—

> So there is one Father, not three Fathers;
> One Son, not three Sons;
> One Holy Ghost, not three Holy Ghosts—

seriously contemplate either a heresy to be contradicted, or a truth to be affirmed; they are merely, as it were, the overflowing of a style so caught with its own manner that it could not stop even when it had reached the limit which was laid down by the sense.[2] There is a poetic fire in its vitals; there are the elements of strophe and antistrophe, chorus and counter-chorus; but in that case we must forego its claims to be considered as a rigid rule of faith, a literal and formal statement of dogmatic propositions.

Unfortunately, however, the polemic substance has

and this false antithesis is one of the internal proofs of the late origin of that apocryphal text.

[1] It is this impression which its public recital often leaves on half-educated or uneducated people, namely, that it is a Creed where 'the 'clerk immediately contradicts what has been said by the clergyman,' or where 'the clergyman and the people quarrel all the way through.' In musical services this disagreeable effect is in a great degree obviated.

[2] Some similar expressions, it is true, occur in St. Augustine's *Treatise on the Trinity*, and a fantastic formula of Phrygian baptism containing a like confusion of thought existed in the third century (Bingham, xi. cap. 3, sect. 4); but the prominence of this doctrine in the Athanasian Creed must be due to some such cause as that above indicated.

been too strong for the poetic form. The Creed is, in spite of its harmonious rhythm, intensely and (as we shall see in speaking of the damnatory clauses) bitterly controversial. If it be 'more devotional than the *Te Deum*,'[1] it is only so in the sense that the 109th Psalm is more devotional than the 51st. It is a 'symbol' in the sense of a military watchword more than in the sense of a Christian pass-word. In comparison with the Apostles', or with the Nicene, Creed, it is evident that every sentence has been put together with the view of combining the utmost amount of purely abstract matter with the least amount of infusion from history or morals. When at the close of the Creed we drop from its own statements into those simple clauses which are borrowed from the earlier confessions, we seem to have passed from the vortex of a whirlpool into the back-water of a still lake.

Its positiveness.

2. In these polemical statements there are two peculiarities—one of form or general intention, one of the particular expressions used. The peculiarity of form or intention has been well described by Dr. Newman.[2] 'The dogma of the Trinity,' he says, 'is 'not called a mystery in the Athanasian Creed. It 'implies a glorying in the mystery, but it is not 'simply a statement of the mystery for the sake of 'its mysteriousness.' This is perfectly true. The author of the Creed does not appear to have had a moment's perplexity as to any difficulty in the

[1] Dr. Newman's *Grammar of Assent*, p. 129. [2] Ibid. pp. 128, 129.

propositions which he was announcing. Modern readers approach the doctrine of the Trinity with a sense of mystery which to the framer of this Creed was quite unknown. To him all was plain. In this respect this Creed is a striking contrast even to the treatise of St. Augustine, from which it is sometimes supposed to have been borrowed. Although even in that work there is but a very slight indication of the more purely modern element of awe, yet there is a profound sense of humility and hesitancy. 'Verius 'cogitatur Deus quam dicitur, verius est quam cogi-'tatur,' is a sentence which softens much in the thorny statements of the African bishop. There is nothing of this diffidence in the Creed of the unknown Frenchman or Spaniard. One only word, as it appears in the English translation, might seem to lean in this direction, and has much encouraged this erroneous notion of its purpose—the word 'incom-'prehensible.'[1] It is probably one of the phrases which most dwells in the mind in connection with the Creed of St. Athanasius; and it has fallen to our lot within twelve months to have seen a severe attack on the Creed for containing a phrase alleged to be so contrary to the simplicity and openness of the Gospel,

[1] Mr. Swainson (p. 22) has called attention to the fact that the Reformers were fatally misled in this as in their general view of the Creed by believing that a Greek translation, first published in 1533, was the original work of Athanasius. It was itself full of errors, which were reproduced in the English translation which we now use. Of these one was the word ἀκατάληπτος, which is stereotyped in our 'incom-'prehensible.'

'Incomprehensible,' a mistranslation of the word immensus.

and on the other hand to have heard a powerful sermon from an eloquent preacher, justifying by this same gross mistranslation the notion that the doctrine of the Trinity was meant to be unintelligible. But in the original Latin there is no such thought. It represents another truth altogether. It is simply '*immensus*'—'unmeasured,' 'not confined to any 'particular place,' and conveys the notion not of the mystery, but of the indefinite extension, of the Divine Nature.[1] The difference between '*immensus*' and 'incomprehensible' indicates the difference between the perfectly comprehensible and intelligible notion of the doctrine of the Trinity, as conceived by the author of the Athanasian Creed, and its inscrutable and unfathomable obscurity, as conceived by modern theologians. It indicates also the extent to which the public recital of the Creed with this misleading word deceives the congregations who hear and the ministers who read it.

3. There are, however, other parts of its language to which this remark applies more fully. The argument of the Creed chiefly turns on the distinction between two words, translated in the English 'sub'stance' and 'person.' It becomes necessary to dwell for a few moments on the meaning of these phrases in the original, whether Greek or Latin. The word 'substance' is the Anglicised form of the Latin word '*substantia*,' which is the rendering of the Greek word

[1] See Ambrose on Luc. ii. 13.

usia (οὐσία). It might have been thought that the more obvious Latin word for this would have been *essentia*; as certainly, at the present day, the natural English word would have been 'essence.' At one time[1] the Western churches even preferred to retain the original Greek word *usia* untranslated. But the fact, however explained, that 'substance' was the word chosen as the rendering of *usia*, has materially coloured the whole aspect of the Creed. Of the meaning of 'essence,' in modern times, we seem to know something; but of the meaning of the word 'substance' we know hardly anything, except in the totally different sense of 'matter,' 'stuff;' which is undoubtedly its signification in modern parlance most frequently. How widely even well-instructed minds can go astray on this very word, is evident from the almost universal mistake into which most Protestants and most Roman Catholics fall in speaking of 'Transubstantiation.' The former in attacking, the latter in defending, the miracle which is supposed to take place in the transformation of the bread and wine, imagine that the visible forms of bread and wine are really, though invisibly, changed into the actual, though invisible, body and blood of Christ. It is well known to any one who has studied the meaning of the words, that according to the true scholastic doctrine nothing of the kind is intended. The outward forms of bread and wine are supposed to remain entirely unchanged;

Various meanings of 'substance.'

[1] St. Basil, *Ep.* 349.

the outward forms of the body and blood of Christ are not supposed to be there either visibly or invisibly. What (it is alleged) does happen is that the invisible ideal or essence (*substance*) of the bread and wine, which never is present to the bodily eye, is changed, not into the visible flesh and blood, but into the invisible ideal or essence (*substance*) of that flesh and blood. But what most Protestants and most Roman Catholics mean by 'the substance' which is supposed to undergo this transformation, is in true scholastic language not 'the substance' but 'the 'accidents;' and the transformation which popular Protestantism and popular Catholicism believe to take place, would by true scholastic divines be called not 'transubstantiation,' but 'transaccidentation.' We have digressed thus far in order to show how on a kindred subject the imagination and intellect of men and of churches may be led astray by the misconception of one of the two chief words used in the Athanasian Creed. What may have been the precise meaning attached to 'substance' as applied to the nature of God, by the author of the Creed, it is difficult to say. All that can be safely affirmed is that, judging by the parallel instance of 'Transubstantiation,' it is in the highest degree improbable that the uneducated— it is in a high degree improbable that even many educated persons—grasp the metaphysical idea either of the Latin '*substantia*,' or of the still more remote Greek '*usia*.' Dr. Newman (than whom no one can be a better judge on such a subject) has said, 'What 'do I know about substance or matter? just as much 'as the greatest philosopher, and that is nothing at all.'[1] To the mass of ordinary persons the word suggests the same idea that it suggested to Tertullian—of corporeal matter. This is the sense in which we most commonly use it, and the extremely subtle character of the scholastic meaning rather encourages the uneducated mind to adopt the more obvious signification.

But this difficulty, whatever it be, is complicated still more by the context in which the word occurs. The phrases '*substantia*' and 'substance' would, if taken in their obvious, literal, etymological sense, be the equivalents of the Greek word *hypostasis*. *Hypostasis* is, in Greek, exactly that *standing under*, that *substratum*, which is expressed in Latin by *substantia*. So, in the New[2] Testament, it is used as equivalent to *usia*, or *essence*. So we are told by St. Jerome that it was used in his time in the schools of philosophers.[3] So it is used in modern Greek[4] philosophical discussions. And so (which is still more important, as bearing on the present controversy) it was used in

Hypostasis.

---

[1] *Apologia*, p. 375. Compare a like train of thought in Dr. Pusey's *Eirenicon*, part iii. pp. 80–83.

[2] In Heb. i. 13, translated 'person;' in Heb. xi. 1, translated 'substance;' but in the original meaning the same.

[3] 'In secular schools *hypostasis* is only another word for *usia*.' (*St. Jerome's Epistles*, 57.)

[4] Thus, in a learned and able article 'On the Unity of Science,' in modern Greek, by our present acccomplished Greek minister, Sir Peter Brailas, *hypostasis* is constantly used in the sense of *substance* or *substratum*.

Identical with 'substance.'

the time of Athanasius himself. At the close of the Nicene Council the Church anathematized those who said that the Son was 'of a different Person' (*hypostasis*) 'or Substance' (*usia*) from the Father, thus implying the identity of the two phrases. It is true that a divergent sense very soon began to form itself. At the Council of Alexandria, A.D. 362, there was an attempt to introduce another definition of *hypostasis*. But Athanasius resisted the attempt, and insisted on leaving the matter in its original vagueness.[1] It is true that St. Basil and St. Gregory of Nyssa shortly after resumed the controversy, and St. Basil[2] undertook the difficult task of explaining away the identity of the two words as used in the Nicene Creed; and a Synodical letter after the Council of Constantinople contains the word *hypostasis* as signifying the three distinctions in the Godhead. But still no Council has ever reversed the decision of the Council of Nicæa, which declares, under an anathema, that Person and Substance—*hypostasis* and *usia*—are the same. It is a remark of Dr. Newman, on this Nicene decision, that 'its language is so obscure that even theologians 'differ about its meaning.' It is, however, obscure not in itself, but because the words employed in it are so variable that with each age they have changed their meaning; and the propositions in which they

[1] It is well known that Athanasius in his own writings avoided even his own phrase *homoüsion*. (Bishop Kaye's *Account of the Council of Nicæa*, p. 57.)
[2] *Ep.* 349.

are used become more uncertain in proportion as their meanings are multiplied.

There is yet one further confusion which should be noticed. Even after the Greeks had, in contravention of the Nicene decision, separated the word *hypostasis* from the word *usia*, the Western theologians could not avoid seeing that the natural Latin translation of it was *substantia*; insomuch that St. Hilary actually thus rendered it, and that in the very treatise on which the Athanasian Creed is founded, St. Augustine says that the Greeks recognised in the Godhead '*tres* '*substantias, unam essentiam.*'

This word, then, which in the original Greek is so deeply identified with *substance*—which was prohibited, under the anathema of the Nicene Council, to be separated from it—which in the Council of Sardica[1] was repeatedly and solemnly asserted to be its equivalent—is the very word which as reproduced in the Latin of the Athanasian Creed is made to be its exact antithesis. On the distinction between the two, as on two opposite poles, the whole controversy of the Creed rolls. Whereas, in the early days of Athanasius it would have been heresy to divide the *hypostasis*, in the Athanasian Creed it is heresy not to divide it. Whereas in the time of Athanasius it was heresy to say that Person (*hypostasis*) and Substance (*usia*) were different, in the Athanasian Creed it is heresy to say that they are the same.

Opposed to 'substance.'

[1] Theodoret, *H. E.* ii. 8.

It is impossible not to sympathise—no one need fear to sympathise on such a matter—with the perplexities of St. Jerome. 'They insist on my recog-'nising three *hypostases*. I ask what these words 'signify. They answer that it means "Three subsist-'" ing persons." I reply that this is my belief. They 'insist that this is not enough, and that I must say '"*hypostasis*." I reply that I fear "*hypostasis*" is 'the same as Substance.' His difficulty was great then; it would have been greater, had he lived now, under the additional complications which fifteen more centuries have added to the confusion. Quintilian and Seneca had protested in vain against the introduction of the word '*substantia*' into philosophy.[1] But its apparition in theology was more perplexing still. And Bacon has well placed it in the list of notions 'unsound,' 'not clear,' 'fantastical,' and 'ill-defined.'

There is, however, within all this coil a yet more intricate entanglement. Not only had the word *hypostasis* in Greek changed its meaning between the time of the Nicene Council and the time of the com-

'Persona:' position of this Creed, but the Latin word '*persona*,'
change of which was used to translate the Greek word *hypostasis*,
meaning. meant something different even from the newly-acquired meaning of *hypostasis* itself; and yet further, the English word '*person*' now means something different both from the Latin word *persona* and from the Greek word *hypostasis*. '*Persona*' is 'a mask—a

[1] See Dean Liddell's admirable *Sermon on the Eucharist*, p. 17.

'character;' just as the Greek word which most nearly corresponds to it (πρόσωπον) is 'a face.' As applied therefore to the Deity, it meant the outward manifestation as distinct from the inward essence of the Supreme Being. By slow degrees the word was transformed into its modern but now almost universal meaning of a separate individual. In earlier English, even as late as Shakspeare, the old meaning of 'character' still lingered ('I then did use the *person* of your father'). Even the form in which it first became fixed as the name of a single individual, 'a parson,' meant to describe him, not in his individual capacity, but in the character or office which he bore. But Locke's definition of it is substantially that which has now taken the place of the ancient meaning: 'A person is 'a thinking, intelligent being, that has reason and 'reflection, and can consider itself as itself—the same 'thinking being in different times and places.' This is the first passage quoted by Johnson in explanation of his own definition of the word: 'Individual, or parti-'cular man or woman.' How entirely remote this is either from the Greek *hypostasis* or the Latin *persona*, it is needless to point out. Yet it is unquestionably the chief idea formed of the word as used in the Athanasian Creed, not only by the uneducated, but even by many of the well-instructed. 'The term '"Person,"' says an able modern advocate of the use of the Creed,[1] 'cannot be employed to denote

'Person:' change of meaning.

---

[1] Liddon's *Bampton Lectures*, 49.

'the distinctions in the Godhead without considerable
'intellectual caution.' The warning is well needed.
Even a deeply learned theologian has been known to
make it a serious charge against another theologian
equally learned, that he did not believe the third
'Person' of the Trinity to be 'a separate Being.' To
believe any one of the 'Persons' to be 'a separate
'being,' as far as the Godhead is concerned, is
obviously in direct contravention to the ancient
meaning of the word; but it is undoubtedly the
natural inference from the fact that 'separate being'
is the modern sense of the word 'person,' which (as
has been seen) in the original language, and even in
older English, meant, it may almost be said, the very
reverse. Nay, the false meaning of the word *Person*
has crept into one of the most important clauses of
the Athanasian Creed itself, in direct contradiction to
the well-known meaning of the original Nicene doctrine.
'We confess,' so the clause now runs, 'every
'Person *by Himself* to be God and Lord.' A recent
defender[1] of the Creed declares that 'this savours of
'heresy,' and he accordingly, to restore the orthodoxy
of the passage, strikes out these important words.
Emmanuel Swedenborg and his followers, who acknowledge
no Person in the Trinity but that of 'the
'Divine Man Jesus Christ,' are yet ardent admirers
of the Athanasian Creed, and claim its sanction for
their doctrine, and are ready to 'demonstrate that all

[1] Swainson on the *Athanasian Creed*, p. 29.

'its contents, even to the very words, are agreeable
'to the truth, *provided* that for a Trinity of Persons,
'we understand a Trinity of Person.' 'With this re-
'servation,' we are told, 'the mind of a Swedenborgian
'may traverse the clauses of that arduous dogma with
'joyful assent and consent.'[1] 'The word "Person,"'
says another of the same school, 'in its proper, true,
'rational, and intelligible meaning is simply a human
'being, a man, and cannot in strictness of speech be
'predicated of the Father or of the Holy Spirit, but
'only of the Lord Jesus Christ. Bearing in mind this
'ordinary and well understood acceptation of the
'term, comprehension of the Athanasian Creed is
'possible and even easy to any mind of education and
'intelligence.'[2] It may be questioned whether this
defence of the Creed will be acceptable to its usual
champions; but it is interesting as showing the utter
divergence of meaning involved in the word on which
the whole document hinges.

This change of the meaning of sacred terminology
is in itself exceedingly interesting, and the study of it
one of the most fruitful fields of theological investiga-
tion. But as regards the public use of the Creed, it
cannot be concealed that such a fact materially affects
its value as a dogmatic guide at the present time. It
may be that the change of the meaning of the words
is of no practical importance. But if it is of no great

[1] White's *Life of Swedenborg*, ii. 115.
[2] *The Athanasian Creed and Modern Thought*, by the Rev. F. M. Gorman, pp. 134–36.

moment whether the ministers who use, and the congregations who hear these antithetical contrasts between 'person' and 'substance,' attach any idea to them, or attach ideas wholly different from that which they represented in the mind of their author; if the chief words employed can only be used 'with con-' siderable intellectual caution'—then the use of public dogmatic statements on these subjects must be estimated accordingly. No doubt there are many statements which are, or must be, misunderstood, or understood in various senses by a mixed congregation; and this is one of the many proofs of the infinite variations of the expression of theological truth. But if there is a supreme importance in using these words, and no others, for the truths in question (and we shall see as we proceed that the author of the Creed certainly was of that opinion), then there is a manifest anomaly[1] in putting into the mouths of ordinary people expressions which they are not only sure to understand amiss, but which are actually so misunderstood by hundreds every time they are spoken. Perhaps these words usually suggest no ideas at all; but (to use the language of an able writer on the subject)—

[1] The expression occurs on two other occasions in the Liturgy. But its use on those occasions is not open to the same objections as in the Athanasian Creed. (1) Because they are merely incidental. (2) Because in them the phrase is not given as the only legitimate formula, but as expressing what in the vast majority of the prayers is expressed through quite other forms. (3) Because it is not, as in the Athanasian Creed, enforced as the one indispensable form under the most awful penalties.

If an ordinary Englishman does attempt to fathom their meaning, he probably understands 'substance' in the sense of matter, and 'person' in the sense of individual, and thus is led by the very Creed, which is to preserve him from error, into the two gravest of all heresies with respect to the Godhead, that the Divine Nature is corporeal, and that there are three Gods.

If the same truth can be conveyed through totally different phrases, then there can be but little ground for the terror which is often expressed at the slightest variation from particular forms of theological expression. It is not denied that underneath these various forms there may be discerned one or more great truths. But these truths may be, and in fact have been, expressed by forms of words, exactly inverting the order and meaning of those used in the 'Creed of ' St. Athanasius.' In the Apostles' Creed neither 'sub-'stance' nor 'person' occurs. In the Nicene Creed, as it now stands, 'substance' has been struck out of one of the two clauses where it once stood, and the clause containing 'person' has been struck out altogether. The very phrase 'Three Persons' is not only not contained in, but is alien to, the original Nicene Theology. If, on the other hand, as Dr. Newman says of the same words used in another sense in the original Creed of Nicæa, 'peasants are bound to be-'lieve them as well as controversialists,'[1] it would seem that unless the peasant has some chance of knowing what it is that they intend to teach, it is

[1] *Grammar of Assent*, p. 142.

26   THE ATHANASIAN CREED.

hardly right to enforce them upon his belief under a threat of the most dreadful penalties; at any rate, such a threat is useless, if he does not know to what precise crime they are intended to apply.

4. This brings us to the parts of the Creed which are even more peculiarly characteristic of it than its poetic rhythm, or its dogmatic statements, although, doubtless, they cannot be altogether separated from either. We refer, of course, to its condemning, or, as they have been for many years called, its 'damna-'tory clauses.' They are peculiar to this Creed, in more senses than one. It is true that anathemas were appended to the original Nicene Creed, and are still appended to every dogma issued by the Roman Catholic Church; but these anathemas have been gradually left more and more in the background. The Nicene anathemas appear, indeed, whenever the Nicene Creed is recited in its original form, as for example (it is believed) in the heretical Churches of Kurdistan and of Egypt. But in the orthodox Greek Church they were, as far as appears, repeated for the last time at the Council of Chalcedon, and the Chalcedonian Fathers adopted in the place of the old Nicene Creed the Confession, which is generally believed to be the work of the Council of Constantinople. From that time, inasmuch as in the orthodox East and the whole Western Church that Creed took the place, and usurped the name, of the older Nicene Creed, the anathemas silently dropped. The reason, perhaps,

why they had never been appended to that enlarged form was, that it was not really the work of the General Council, but rather of some individual theologian—whether Epiphanius or Gregory of Nyssa—who, influenced by milder temperament or by the feeling that he had not adequate authority, declined to insert them. The Apostles' Creed—possibly for a similar reason—viz., that it never was confirmed by a Council—has never had the anathemas at all. The Athanasian Creed, therefore (if we except the confessions of the Coptic and Nestorian Churches, which, as has been already noticed, are believed still to use the anathemas of the Nicene Creed), is the only public confession of faith to which such curses are now attached.[1]

But the peculiarity of the Athanasian anathemas is more remarkable yet. They are not, as in the case of the old Nicene Creed, appended as a mere separable adjunct, but are firmly incorporated at the beginning, the middle, and the end of the Creed, so as to form its most prominent features, both to the eye and to the ear. Its very title is taken, not from the truths

Peculiarity of the Damnatory Clauses.

---

[1] It may be observed as a proof of the gradual extermination of these anathemas by a more Christian feeling, that in the Greek Church the service of Orthodox Sunday, in which all the heretics were anathematized by name, is now generally discontinued. One of the earlier forms of the Roman dogma of the Pope's infallibility had also, by a momentary concession to Christian truth and charity, dropped the anathema. It is, however, reinstated in that which was actually adopted by the Vatican Council on July 18, 1870.

which it proclaims, but from the penalties which it invokes on those who deny them. It is not the '*Credo*,' but the '*Quicunque Vult.*' And further, these denunciations, unlike those appended to the Nicene Creed or to modern dogmas (which are contained in a single word, and that an exceedingly general one), are stated with the utmost particularity, and applied with the utmost universality. Instead of the vague expression , 'the Church anathematizes,' which might, perhaps, mean no more than a temporal and temporary excommunication, is the awful phrase, '*He shall without doubt perish everlastingly.*' Instead of the indefinite expression, 'Let him be anathema,' is the extreme and penetrating individualization, '*Whosoever* will be saved,' '*Every one* shall perish.' Instead of the reference to the Creed generally, is the particularization of every part of it: 'Which unless a ' man do keep *whole and undefiled ;*' '*in all* things, as ' is aforesaid,' '*necessary* to everlasting salvation that ' he believe rightly;' and the repetition of the corresponding phrases at each turn of the Creed,[1] as has been well said, clenches and nails every single part together into one indissoluble whole.[2]

[1] This is well put in Mr. Lyttelton's excellent letter to the *Guardian* newspaper, Feb. 14, 1870. He adds an instance which shows that this terrific penalty is even in our day practically applied to every part. ' I ' once heard a distinguished clergyman make the little children in the ' village school repeat the damnatory clauses at each sentence of the ' Creed, and I could not deny that logically he was justified in so doing.'

[2] One remedy proposed for the better understanding of these clauses is, that they should be re-translated. It is maintained that '*quicunque*

So remarkable a variation from the usual form of creeds must have had some peculiar origin. It may be that the author of the Creed—Victricius, or some one like Victricius—accused of heresy himself, took this fearful mode of clearing his reputation. 'Many 'a man,' says a Spanish proverb, 'has won for himself 'the name of a saint by calling others necromancers;' and it may well be that a person of suspected orthodoxy may have thought this tremendous repudiation of heresy his only safety. At the Council of Nicæa, the severest humiliation to which the Arian bishops

'vult salvus esse' should be rendered, 'whosoever *wishes to be in a state* '*of salvation*;' that '*ita sentiat*' should be not '*must* thus think,' but '*let* him thus think.' The proposal of such a remedy suggests three inevitable remarks. 1. The difference of meaning, whatever it be, is but slight, and there still remain the no less terrible clauses, 'he shall 'without doubt perish everlastingly,' and 'he cannot be saved.' 2. If the difference were important, it is an acknowledgment that the Creed as now retained and recited conveys a meaning essentially false on a subject of infinite gravity. 3. Whatever may be the obscurity of the damnatory clauses in English, it is not to be compared to the obscurities of the English rendering of the dogmatic parts of the Creed in the words 'incomprehensible,' 'Person,' and 'substance,' and the avowedly heretical version of one of the most important of the doctrinal clauses, 'we must believe every Person by Himself to be God and Lord.' If the Creed is to be re-translated in the portions which are the most intelligible, much more it must be re-translated in those which are the most obscure. Such a re-translation would indeed be a revolution in our treatment of the Creed. But, as we shall see, it would not affect our present and past use of it.

It would surely be a better plan, as was proposed in a letter addressed to the *Guardian*, that the Creed should always be recited in the original language. If unintelligible, it would then, at any rate, not be misleading.

were subjected was signing even the brief anathemas then in use to condemn their brethren: how much more efficacious would be the terrible asseverations of the '*Quicunque Vult*'? Or it may be that they express some peculiar outburst of triumph over a theological enemy—such as, if Waterland's date of the reception of the Creed be correct, would have been the victory of Clovis over the Visigoths; or, if Mr. Ffoulkes's conjecture be accepted, the assertion of Western orthodoxy over Eastern heresy, at the time of Charlemagne.

Whatever be the explanation, the fact imparts to the Creed a unique historical interest. It serves the purpose of one of those landmarks left in levelling ground to show the site of a former entrenchment. It is invaluable as a relic or fragment of ancient times, the more because out of keeping with the surrounding objects. But the more curious as an historical monument, the less suitable does it become for general and perpetual use. And this is to be observed, in proportion as the policy which the anathemas represent is not only antiquated, but is now almost universally regarded as one which we should least desire to revive. Athanasius himself, as we have seen, could not by any possibility have attached these anathemas to forms of expression which he deprecated. Even the peremptory statements with which the Creed opens and closes —'The Catholic Faith is this,' 'This is the Catholic 'Faith'—would have been in his eyes a certain mark of Cataphrygian heresy.[1] Augustine, as we have seen, spoke with a hesitation and diffidence the very reverse of the positiveness of the pseudo-Athanasian anathemas. But the passion for punishing erroneous opinions with the most frightful pains both in this world and the next grew rapidly. Undoubtedly and unhappily, whether the Creed was composed in the fifth century or the eighth, these clauses expressed the feeling of many of the ablest theologians of the time—that formal orthodoxy was the indispensable passport to salvation, formal heresy the inevitable forerunner of everlasting destruction. The particular shape of the Athanasian anathemas was, indeed, exceptional, but the temper which they express belonged to the age. They awakened, they could awaken, no horror, no distrust, in those who had not the slightest scruple in slaughtering and burning alive the very persons whom these clauses were supposed to condemn. The modern qualifications forced by the charity and justice of later days upon these curses would no more occur to the framers or the recipients of this Creed from the fifth to the sixteenth century, than they did in withholding St. Louis, or Isabella the Catholic, or Cranmer, from committing heretics to the flames; or in withholding even Augus-

---

[1] 'Speaking of the Arians,' Athanasius says, 'they have not written, " so we believe," but in this form, " *This Catholic Faith is published.*" ' By adding the word " *Catholic*," they fall into the transgression of the ' Cataphrygians, so as to say with them, " The Christian Faith was ' " first revealed to, and begins from us." '

tine from consigning to endless torments the souls of unbaptized children ; or Dante from lodging all heathens and heretics in the circles of the *Inferno*.

Hincmar, in the ninth century, submitted to the dying Gotteschalk the dogmatic parts of the Creed as a condition of absolution or of Christian sepulture. It did not need that he should recite the damnatory clauses. The refusal of the rites of the Church, the contumely of treating the unfortunate prisoner as an outcast, was, in that age, their equivalent.[1] Hildegarde, the Abbess and Prophetess of the twelfth century, rightly interpreted the general feeling when she explained them as saying that any 'who wished to be 'saved must hold the faith lest he be cast into hell.'

But as they were probably the parts of the Creed which most commended it to the Church, so long as this sentiment lasted, so they were the parts which were the first to rouse difficulties respecting its acceptance, in proportion as a more Christian sentiment sprang up.

There is some faint sign of hesitation respecting them in earlier times. There is one instance of the omission of three of the offensive phrases,[2] and Wycliffe[3] seems to have had a momentary doubt

---

[1] Swainson, *Athanasian Creed*, p. 71.

[2] In one of the manuscript copies of the exposition ascribed to Venantius Fortunatus, the two damnatory clauses in the middle, and one at the beginning, are omitted. The rest are retained. *Ibid.* pp. 67-70.

[3] Wycliffe's *Exposition of the 'Quicunque Vult.'* St. Thomas

as to requiring the belief of every statement in the Creed as a condition of salvation. But these compunctions were long in making themselves felt. The cruel necessity under which the Reformers felt themselves of vindicating their orthodoxy whenever they could, and the savage temper against heretics which the first Protestant Churches inherited from the Middle Ages, stifled many questionings which might otherwise have arisen in the earlier days of the Reformation. It was not till the middle of the seventeenth century, that the protests of the best and wisest of the English clergy began to be raised against the damnatory clauses. From that time they have been either considered as sufficient reason for laying aside the use of the Creed itself, or have been subjected to explanations which have entirely changed their meaning. 'It seems very 'hard,' says Bishop Jeremy Taylor, 'to put uncha-'ritableness into the Creed, and so to make it become 'an article of faith.' 'The damning clauses in St. 'Athanasius' Creed,' says Chillingworth, 'are most 'false, and also in a high degree schismatical 'and presumptuous.' (Letter to Sheldon, Sept. 21, 1635.) Baxter, in signing the Articles, expressly excepted 'assent to the damnatory clauses of the

Aquinas (*Summa Theologiæ*, Secunda secundæ, quæst. 2. art. 8), though with some interesting remarks on the distinction between implicit and explicit faith, is positive as to the necessity for salvation of accepting all the usual statements respecting the Trinity.

'Athanasian Creed.' (Orme's Life, i. 489.) 'The 'account given of Athanasius' Creed appears to me in 'no wise satisfactory,' says Archbishop Tillotson; 'I 'wish we were well rid of it.' (Life of Burnet.) 'The 'most eminent men of the English Church,' says Bishop Burnet (on Article viii.), 'as far back as the 'memory of all that I know can go up, confine them 'to such as stifled their own convictions.'[1] Archbishop Secker 'thought it a pity they had not been originally 'omitted' (vi. 220). Bishop Marsh, 'though he argued 'against the inference deduced from the anathemas, 'did not mean to defend them.' Professor Burton regarded them as 'essentially different and uncon-'nected with the Creed;' and thought 'that Christian 'charity and humility would wish that they were 'not retained and read publicly.' (Sermon on Mark xvi. 16.) Professor Hey, besides other modifications, proposes to substitute, 'He that hath ears 'to hear let him hear' (iii. 118). Dr. Arnold said, 'I do not believe the damnatory clauses of the 'Athanasian Creed under any justification given of 'them, except such as substitutes for them proposi-'tions of a wholly different character.' (Life, p. 749.) Bishop Lonsdale openly condemned them, and was emphatically silent during their repetition in the public service. (Denison's 'Life of Bishop Lonsdale,' p. 113.)

Coleridge (to take one example of an eminent lay theologian) says, 'This Creed, if not persecuting,

[1] This probably refers to the Rubric suggested, but not adopted, in 1689.

'which I will not discuss, certainly contains harsh 'and ill-conceived language.' (Table Talk, p. 45.)

III. Such are the peculiarities of this famous Creed. Each one of them, whilst it enhances its value as an historical monument, diminishes its value as a guide of theological thought, and yet more its practical value as a devotional formulary. It might be questionable whether it was worth while to retain in the teeth of the decrees of two General Councils, a Creed which obtained admittance under the name of Athanasius, now universally acknowledged to have been a misnomer; at least, nothing short of extraordinary intrinsic merit would justify such a procedure. It might be questionable whether it was worth while to retain as a public formulary a Creed, of which most of the essential words are understood by the common people in a sense very different from their original intention, and of which the chief champions of the Creed have said that they 'ought 'not to be employed without considerable intellectual 'caution,' or that 'nothing at all is known' about their meaning. It becomes most of all questionable when these words, thus ambiguous in themselves, are enforced under anathemas the most terrible and plain that human language admits, and which have now universally ceased (in their obvious sense) to be believed.

1. There are, however, still further anomalies consequent on its use in the Church of England. Here, again, there is an historical peculiarity which, con-

sidered in an antiquarian point of view, may be worth preserving. Ours is the only Church in Christendom where it is ordered to be recited publicly in mixed congregations; perhaps in consideration of the peculiarly English practice of reciting it, in the Middle Ages, daily. In the Roman Church, which limits its recitation, as a general rule, to conventual and monastic worship,[1] it is never, or hardly ever, recited in public. It is never recited in the Eastern Churches, which, so far as they receive it at all, only receive it with one of its chief Articles omitted, and as a private act of devotion. It is never, or hardly ever, recited[2] in the Lutheran, Belgic, or Bohemian Churches, which retain it in their confessions of faith, nor in the Reformed Churches of France, Switzerland, or Germany, which have not received it in any sense; nor in the Presbyterian Churches of Scotland, nor even in the most highly orthodox of the Nonconformist Churches in England. Further, it was formally rejected both from the Thirty-nine Articles and from the English Liturgy by the Protestant Episcopal Church of the United States. This rejection assumes the most significant aspect when considered in its relation to the law of the English Church. It had been first proposed in the American Convention to reject both the Nicene and Athanasian Creeds. The English

[1] A mystical reason is assigned for this obscure position by St. Thomas Aquinas.
[2] Professor Hey says that it is recited twice a year in the Swedish Church. (*Lectures*, iii. 117.)

archbishops, to whom application had been made for the consecration of the American bishops, demurred, and announced that their course 'must depend on the 'answer they would receive to what they had written.'[1] On the Nicene Creed the American Convention gave way, but it insisted on excluding the Athanasian Creed, and the English archbishops accordingly, under a special statute passed for the occasion, and with the full authority of the English Church and State, gave the Episcopal succession to a Church which had deliberately given notice to them of its rejection of this Creed. In our own time, in spite of this rejection, the bond of union has been drawn closer still; and any clergyman ordained by an American bishop, without subscribing or adhering in any sense to the Athanasian Creed, and with a determination not to use it, may yet by recent legislation minister and preach in the Church of England.

2. A lesser point, peculiar to the English Church (at any rate as compared with the Roman Church, which preserves it in the original Latin), is that great as are its disadvantages under any circumstances, it has for three centuries been presented to the English public in language which is sometimes inaccurate even to heresy. Some of these errors result from the compilers of our Liturgy having been deceived into acceptance of a Greek version of the Creed as the

---

[1] See the whole story carefully given by 'Presbyter Academicus' in *Macmillan's Magazine*, November 1869.

original; such for example as the substitution already noticed of '*incomprehensible*' for '*infinite*,' the substitution of 'believe *rightly*' for 'believe *faithfully*;' the insertion of the heretical words '*every person by Himself* to be God and Lord;' the use of the word '*dividing*' for '*separating*' the substance. Some have crept in from the preponderating influence of Luther; such as the word '*must* thus think' for 'let him think;' and '*none is greater or less*' for 'nothing greater or less,' an expression which, if less intelligible, is more Biblical. To these must be added the grossest of all—the use (as we have seen) of the modern word 'Person' as the equivalent of a phrase of essentially different meaning. Whatever may be the use of the Creed in the future of the English Church, it seems difficult to defend in the past the public recital of a document confessedly calculated, by these numerous errors, to mislead in almost every verse on subjects which are pronounced in the Creed itself to be of the most tremendous significance. The 'Creed of St. Athanasius,' as adopted by the Church of England, is the English translation, not the unknown and unseen original; just as the Collects of the English Church are accepted, not in their Latin, but their English form. And it is this 'imperfect and corrupted version'[1] which alone has been presented to the English public for three hundred years. Whether its retranslation is possible or advisable is another question. In its present, which is

---

[1] Swainson on *The Athanasian Creed*, p. 37.

its only legal form, it is condemned from beginning to end by the very proposal. It is not, as in the case of the existing Authorized Version of the Bible, where the general sense is retained in spite of errors in detail. Here the errors affect its vital points.

3. Yet further, in the English Church itself the present usage of general recitation is comparatively of modern growth. What may have been the case before its true authorship was known, and before the scruples had arisen against its anathemas, cannot be certainly known; but from the close of the seventeenth century there can be little doubt that it has been frequently omitted in the Church Service. Its unfitness for such use was so generally felt, that (according to Tillotson's famous expression of 'charity being above rubrics') the rubric was neglected and charity prevailed. Excellent laymen have been frequently known to shut the Prayer-book the moment that the Creed began. King George III., on one occasion in the Chapel Royal, is said to have closed the book with such emphasis that for many years the Creed was omitted. The late Bishop Blomfield on coming to the parish of Bishopsgate, finding that it had not been read there within the memory of man, did not revive the use; and it thus happened that he passed through his clerical life without having publicly recited it. We have been told by a venerable dignitary, now far advanced in years, that when he first took Holy Orders more than fifty years ago in

a western diocese, the Creed seemed to be fast dying out. It was not used in ten churches of the diocese besides the cathedral, and he himself never had occasion to join in it. Another curious illustration of the same fact occurs in a midland town, where in 1761 a benefaction was left to those of the churches 'where the Athanasian Creed was recited'—an evident indication that the eccentric donor hoped by this means to secure the continuance of a perishing usage. It was not till the movement of the Oxford school in 1834, for putting in force all the obsolete rubrics of the Church, that the rubric enjoining the frequent use of the Athanasian Creed revived amongst the rest. Doubtless it was peculiarly acceptable to the 'fierce 'thoughts'[1] which at that time animated the leaders of the High Church party against all tolerant and liberal views. Its revival remains one of the chief monuments of the movement which in later days has issued in what is called 'Ritualism;' and as such it comes before the public not simply as an offensive usage, which for the first time seeks to be relaxed, but as an obsolete usage which, having been relaxed, has for the last thirty years begun to be re-enforced.

Nor has the revival of a Creed which had thus become virtually dead been accompanied by a general acquiescence, such as alone could render it desirable. It may be that there are more who sympathise, or think they sympathise with it, than in former times.

[1] Newman's *Apologia*, pp. 97, 120, 131.

Of these we will speak presently. But of those who loudly complain or silently protest the number has increased in proportion. There are devout Christians who shrink from attending the great festivals of the Church, because they know that on these days they will have their most sacred thoughts of peace and reverence disturbed by expressions which they hear 'with repugnance and horror.' There are parish churches, such as have been graphically described by an eminent pastor, as of his own experience—'As 'soon as the recital of the Creed begins the most 'thoughtful and devout of the parishioners make it the 'signal for sitting down in silence. The rest of the 'congregation soon follow their example; the re-'sponses quaver and fail, and at last no one is left 'to carry them on but the children of the choir; and 'so out of the mouths of babes and sucklings proceed 'those terrible denunciations which they are not ex-'pected to believe, against opinions which they do 'not understand, nor were intended to understand.' The evil is aggravated by the fact that even when the Creed is read, not sung, it is not the clergyman but the congregation to whose lot falls the duty of repeating these withering declarations; and when it is sung, the whole Creed necessarily devolves on the choir, that is usually on laymen, who are for the most part unaccustomed to the explanations by which the more educated clergy deprive the anathemas of their point.

4. We have noticed incidentally the anomalous position in which the use of the Creed places the English Church in regard to the American Episcopal Church. There is another Communion in regard to which the recitation of the Athanasian anathemas in the Church of England is still more difficult to maintain.

When the Creed was discussed in 1689, Burnet urged 'that it condemned the Greek Church, which 'yet we defend.' This was an argument which at that time was likely to have but little practical weight even with the High Churchmen, to whom it was addressed. The Greek Church was then so remote from English view (only brought to sight for a moment, now and then, by the communications of Cyril with Laud, or of Peter the Great with Burnet himself) that no lively impression could be made by pointing out that the anathemas were directed against a body of Christians with which practically the English Church had no intercourse. But now the case is materially altered. Not only has the English Church, and the High Church school in particular, turned with unusual ardour towards friendly communication with the Eastern Churches, but a well-known Greek prelate (the Archbishop of Syra) has received the most brotherly welcome from ecclesiastics of various shades of opinion, but especially of the type of those who profess the warmest attachment to the 'Creed of St. 'Athanasius.' Now, if there be one thing more than another certain of this Creed, it is that it alone, of all the older confessions of faith, contains, as an integral part of its teaching, the clauses respecting the Double Procession [1] of the Holy Ghost, which formed the main doctrinal point of rupture between the Eastern and Western Churches: and that, consequently, the anathemas which condemn those who do not hold its statement of the Catholic faith 'whole and un-'defiled,' strike at every individual of the Eastern Church who still continues to deny that doctrine.

That this is so appears from the appeals to the Athanasian Creed, which first bring it prominently within the view of ecclesiastical history. The first notices of it—perhaps in the fifth and sixth centuries, certainly in the ninth, twelfth, thirteenth, and fifteenth [2] —are such as prove incontestably that it was its assertion of this particular dogma which chiefly commended it, and that its anathemas were then specially directed against the Greek Church, with which at those periods the Latin Church was engaged in deadly war. It was, as Mr. Harvey well remarks, 'the master-word in the dark contests between the 'East and West.' The clause regarding the Double Procession was considered to be so fatal a stumbling-block in the way of the Greeks, that they, when taunted with its being the work of Athanasius,

---

[1] These clauses seem to belong to the ninth century. See Swainson, p. 70.

[2] Waterland, iv. 259, 221, 150, 152, 156, 158, 161.

retorted that he could only have written it when he was drunk.[1] This also appears from the fact that in a Greek translation of the Creed, which, as above noticed, is occasionally inserted in Eastern books of devotion, this clause is studiously omitted, although leaving the context maimed and meaningless without it. The fact is, that the controversy respecting the Double Procession is almost the only one which now survives—even if it may be said to survive—out of the technical phraseology which forms the basis of the Athanasian Creed. Anyone who reads Dr. Donaldson's defence of this Confession in his 'Christian Or-'thodoxy,' will see that in his view, which has been recently adopted by those who wish to retain its use, modern thought of all kind on this question, whether philosophical or theological, whether what is denounced as Rationalist or Unitarian, is altogether outside and beyond the propositions contained in the Creed, or, if within them at all, rather favoured than otherwise. All the various forms of modern speculation on the Trinity spring from an atmosphere of thought, and form a vocabulary of theology altogether subsequent and alien to that which gives to the Athanasian Creed

[1] Gibbon (c. 37) has not quite correctly stated this. He puts this remark into the mouth of Gennadius, the Patriarch of Constantinople. It is not the remark of Gennadius, but his description (apparently depreciatory, as might be expected from his partiality to the Latin Church) of what the Greeks, his countrymen, said of the clause in question. 'They are not ashamed to say that the holy Athanasius was 'drunk, and, when he was writing this, full of wine.' (As quoted by Petavius, *Theol. Dogm.* vii. c. 8.)

its meaning and its intention.¹ It is reported that the eminent Nonconformist minister, Dr. Price, used to say of the Athanasian Creed, that it was but ' Soci-' nianism disguised.' It seems a paradox, but there is some ground for the remark. The truths concerning the Unity of God which Unitarianism teaches are taught by the Creed with a force and clearness which cannot be mistaken. When it is sung in our cathedrals the whole power of the music is thrown into those passages which assert the Divine Unity. But the truths concerning the distinctions in the Godhead on which Trinitarianism dwells are taught by the Creed in words which, as we have seen, have changed their meaning with each succeeding age, and which by those who defend them are accepted only 'with con-' siderable intellectual caution,' or with a reservation that 'nothing at all is known' of their true meaning. The Biblical doctrine of the Unity of God is stated in words which most readers can understand. The Biblical doctrine of the Trinity is stated in words which every uneducated reader misunderstands. And so it has come to pass that whilst the Athanasian anathema fails to hit those whom its admirers desire

---

[1] In a charge of the late lamented Bishop of Calcutta, he observes on the peculiarly Oriental character of the heresies against which the Athanasian Creed protests. This is an additional proof of its irrelevance to the more recent speculations of the West. It may be added in passing that the repugnance of this excellent Prelate to the enforced use of the Athanasian Creed (however much he was anxious to allay the scruples provoked by it) continued unchanged to the end of his life.

it to hit, it strikes with its whole severity those whom they wish to except. The Arian controversy, properly so called, expired with the fall of the Visigothic kingdoms. The Monophysite and Monothelite controversies had either not come into existence (if we take Waterland's view) when the Creed was first composed, or (if we take Mr. Ffoulkes's view) were too remote to be within its vision. Nestorianism, against which one of its clauses seems to be aimed, no doubt still exists in the mountains of Kurdistan. This, however, is too far away to be worth taking into practical consideration. But the controversy on the Double Procession, if exciting but a faint interest in the West, still agitates the minds of the ecclesiastics of Constantinople, of Athens, and of Moscow; and whether as a point of honour, or as a point of doctrine, they will die but never surrender this ancient bone of contention. Against this, therefore, the anathemas continue fresh and green as ever; and, whilst it is perfectly reasonable that we in the English Church might forbear to press the interpolated clause, as it exists unguarded by anathemas, in the Creed of Constantinople, we cannot, without manifest (though happy) inconsistency, forbear to press it, when enforced under such terrific penalties as those laid down in the 'Creed of St. Athanasius,' so long as those anathemas are actively defended or publicly rehearsed in English churches. The plaintive remark of Bishop Lonsdale was only too well founded: 'That the Atha-

'nasian Creed was intended to exclude the Greek 'Church, I admit with sorrow.' (Life, p. 113.) And the accompanying extract from a perplexed clergyman of the Church of England, extracted from the *Church Times*, proves how practical is the Greek difficulty in the eyes of some of those who would be the warmest adherents of the Athanasian Creed :—

It is not easy to come from our stirring Whitsuntide services without—shall I dare to say it?—a hearty zeal for the co-equality of the Spirit with the Father and the Son, and, I must add, a righteous indignation towards those professed members of the Anglican Church who, by the excision of the *Filioque*, would not only cut her off from the whole Communion of the West, from the eighth century forward, but commit her to the essentially erroneous position of the inferiority of the Son and the Spirit to the Father. The echo of the magnificent sentences of the Athanasian Creed, that thunder music of theology, is still pealing in our ears, 'Such as the Father is, such is the Son, and such is the Holy Ghost,' and yet we are to be told that the Father is not only Fountain of Deity in the sense of being First in order, as all Catholics maintain, but is the exclusive Source from which alone both the Son and the Holy Ghost derive existence. And priests of the Church of England, who stand committed by every tie of faith and honour to the Procession from the Father and the Son, venture to denounce wrath and woe upon the Anglican Communion if she does not stultify herself (I cannot speak less plainly) by cutting herself off from the Ante-Reformation Church, from the Faith of a thousand years, and so openly proclaim what in popular apprehension cannot fall short of practical Sabellianism. The Eastern Church has never accepted a certain logical and inevitable consequence of the belief in the Triune Godhead. Nor had the Apostolic, nor had the Church of the fourth and fifth centuries. Granted. That does not affect the Eastern Church's life, though that, and the non-use of the Athanasian Creed, does probably greatly impair her spiritual energies. But to go back from, to put away, practically to condemn this logical deduction, after having accepted it for a thousand years together, would be indeed to depart from the Faith once delivered to the Saints. For that implies essential co-equality.

The plain truth is that the Greek hypothesis is essentially semi-Arian, though I am as far from imputing semi-Arianism to the Eastern as to the Ancient Church. The notion at the bottom of this hypothesis is, that if not in time, at least in eternity, the Father was first alone, and then developed, so to speak, the Son and the Holy Ghost. But this is not so, this is utterly irreconcilable with the Catholic Faith. For the Trinity in Unity was complete from all eternity, the Son ever begotten, the Holy Ghost ever proceeding. The cry of Arians and semi-Arians was always for antiquity! and this naturally so, because the early Fathers had expressed themselves (as Petavius has shown) illogically and incorrectly. This could not well be otherwise. And since the decrees of Councils are appealed to as forbidding all further development, we must needs ask, how should the Faith of the Church have been crystallised either at Nicæa or Constantinople? What legitimate power could any Council have so to bind future ages as to say to the rising tide of Catholic discernment, 'Thus far, and no further'?

Our forefathers could not and would not accept a Creed which, logically interpreted, struck at the root of the Essential Deity both of the Son and of the Spirit. It was Catholic instinct which protested, and righteous zeal for the honour of God the Son, and of God the Holy Ghost, and

CONDEMNATION OF THE EASTERN CHURCHES. 49

these would be satisfied with nothing short of the distinct proclamation of the mighty truth. Eternal honour then to Charlemagne, one of the greatest, if not the greatest, of earthly rulers, for his faithful service in this matter, as in his warfare against image-worship also.

But that Anglicans should suffer themselves to argue against the binding Creeds of their own Church, this appears to me to be quite insufferable. 'The Father is made of 'none, neither created nor begotten. The Son is of the 'Father alone, not made, nor created, but begotten. The 'Holy Ghost is of the Father and of the Son, neither made, 'nor created, nor begotten, but proceeding.'

Such a strong expression of opinion, whether right or wrong, shows that whatever language of alarm is used concerning Sabellians, Apollinarians, or Arians, can be used, and has been used, respecting the Greeks. And of late years, whenever any approximation has been made towards the Eastern Churches, there have always been those who have publicly pointed out, and hailed the indication, that by such friendly overtures the anathemas of the Athanasian Creed, are, as regards the English Church, virtually repealed. In this, the most signal instance of their application, they have been, by these kindly acts, declared to be false and irrelevant. And therefore, as the Greek Church itself has wisely abandoned its ancient practice of solemnly anathematizing the Churches of the West, so it is not too much to be expected that the Church of England at least—whatever may be done by the Church of Rome—shall abandon the practice of launching its

E

anathemas fourteen times a year against the Churches of the East. Vain endeavours are from time to time made to prove that Eastern Christendom is excepted from their operation, because, as is alleged, the Double Procession of the Athanasian Creed may be interpreted to mean the Single Procession of the Greeks; or because, as it is also alleged, the anathemas leap over this particular clause, and leave it intact. But such arguments are tantamount to giving up the Creed altogether, inasmuch as they simply assert that the Creed cannot express its own dogma correctly, and that any particular opinions denounced in it may, at the discretion of individuals, be exempted from its anathemas.

Arguments in favour of retaining the use of the Creed.

IV. It may be well, before we reach the conclusion, to sum up some of the arguments that have been used in favour of a Creed which, whatever else may be said for or against it, unquestionably occupies a singular and exceptional position.

Its historical curiosity.

Its historical value has been sufficiently set forth. Its use is a relic of the age of Charlemagne, perhaps of Clovis, perhaps even of Odoacer or Alaric; not, in any ordinary use of the words, a 'creed of the saints, ' and anthem of the blest,' but a war-song of an unknown author—an interesting example at once of the endeavour of Latin Theology to grasp Byzantine metaphysics, and of Christian speculation to fortify itself with barbarian curses. Nothing else exists like it in the English Prayer-book. If it disappears, we shall

ITS DISADVANTAGES.   51

have lost, for good or evil, a familiar memorial of the old days of fierce haters and plain speakers.

It is also a relic of times before the modern controversies which distract the Church had sprung up. It defines carefully what is and, therefore, what is not the Catholic faith. It declares that heresy consists in denying or modifying certain expressions which it states to be absolutely essential respecting the Three Hypostases and the One Substance of the Divine Being. According to the Athanasian Creed, Pelagianism is not contrary to the Catholic Faith, nor any of the numerous theories that have sprung up, on one side or the other, respecting Justification. Nor, again, is any theory respecting Biblical Inspiration, or respecting the Atonement, or the nature of the Devil, or Baptismal Regeneration, or the Real Presence, or the Sacraments at all, reckoned by the Athanasian Creed as parts 'of the Catholic Faith.' If, on one side, this venerable confession may be narrow and severe, and, on the other side, meagre and defective, yet, to a critical and liberal mind, it is more free and comprehensive than many modern confessions, whether of Rome or Westminster, of the Wesleyan Conference or of the Evangelical Alliance. *Its latitude in regard to modern controversies.*

It may be asked, then, if it has these advantages, and if its most offensive features are constantly explained away even by those who profess to admire them, why it should cease to occupy its present conspicuous place in our public services? The answer *Its evils.*

has already been in part given. It is a creed without authority—constantly and necessarily misunderstood —and involving the Church which continues to enforce it in endless anomalies and contradictions. It may be added, further, that in the damnatory clauses, which are almost the only parts peculiar to this Creed which are commonly understood in their original sense, it tends to keep alive two evil passions of the old theological Adam, which it has been one of the chief aims of our Divine Redeemer to subdue and extirpate.

Exaltation of orthodox belief into the first of virtues.

One is the tendency to exalt correct belief into the first of virtues, and to consider erroneous belief as the worst of crimes. A creed which asserts, in the most emphatic language, that, in order to be 'saved' (whatever sense we attach to that word), it is 'before all ' things necessary to hold the Catholic Faith,' can hardly be said to be of the spirit of Him who declared, ' Not every one that saith unto me Lord, Lord, shall ' enter into the kingdom of heaven, but he that doeth ' the will of my Father which is in heaven;' or of His Apostles, who proclaimed, 'In every land he that feareth ' God and doeth righteousness is accepted of Him;' or ' Circumcision availeth nothing, nor uncircumcision, ' but the keeping of the commandments of God;' or, ' He that doeth righteousness is righteous.' Even as regards doctrine we may doubt whether ' before' the statements respecting ' Substance' and ' Person' it may not be more 'necessary, before all things,' to believe that God is Love, that Charity is the greatest of human virtues, that there are Two Great Commandments, and that to fulfil these is more important even than holding the Catholic Faith. Other expressions of another kind may doubtless be found in other parts of the Bible. Let them be fairly considered. But they are not its key-note, or its general tone. They belong to modes of feeling, on their face more or less transitory, more or less exceptional. The text which is most commonly adduced in support of the damnatory clauses is Mark xvi. 16: —'He that believeth and is baptized shall be saved; 'but he that believeth not shall be damned.' But this is an exception which proves the rule. For first, the belief here spoken of is not the belief in a series of intricate antithetical propositions respecting the Hypostatic union; it is not even (as is sometimes supposed by a confusion between this and the parallel place in St. Matthew) a belief in the Threefold Name itself acknowledged by all the various sects of Christendom, but simply a belief in 'the Gospel' ('Go 'preach the Gospel'), in its largest and widest acceptation, which would even more evidently include every shade of Christian, orthodox or heretical. Secondly, the word '*damned*,' when taken (as in this argument it always is taken) in the well-known sense in which it is used in the coarse[1] colloquialism of modern English,

The irrelevancy of Mark xvi. 16.

---

[1] A singular instance of this occurs in a treatise by a learned and amiable divine of the Roman Catholic Church (*The Priest and his*

is not a proper representation of the old English word, which once meant no more than 'condemned,' and thus falls altogether short of the unqualified and extreme severity of the Athanasian denunciations. And thirdly, if even with these limitations the passage has a harsh sound, unlike the usual utterances of the Evangelical teaching, the critical knowledge of the MSS. of the New Testament has shown that it is not a part of St. Mark's Gospel, but an addition by another hand, of which the external coincides with the internal evidence in proving its later origin. When,[1] therefore, this passage is cited by theologians as the 'statement of our Lord Himself,' 'our Lord's 'own anathema,' in defence of the Athanasian curses, they in fact surrender their cause: for they rest their position on a text which is, first, inapplicable; secondly, mistranslated; thirdly, apocryphal.

The other evil is the tendency to apply warnings which, if true at all, can be taken only in the most general, and in the most qualified terms, to particular classes and particular persons to whom we may happen to entertain a peculiar distaste. It is sometimes said

---

Mission, by the Very Rev. Canon Oakeley, p. 92), where he pleads the false Protestant translation against the more correct rendering of his own Douay version, and urges the text, without the slightest indication of its apocryphal character, as a decisive proof of the 'damnation' ('in 'its unveiled awfulness') of intellectual perversity.

[1] The case is well put in *A Few More Words on the Athanasian Creed*, by 'Presbyter Academicus,' in *Macmillan's Magazine*, November 1869, p. 40.

that there is no more harm in using these clauses against certain opinions, than in using general denunciations, whether in Biblical or in common language, against certain vices. But it is obvious that the parallel fails in almost every particular. Even with regard to warnings against sin, it is certain that neither Scripture nor experience justifies us in using language so positive, so individual, so unqualified, as that which is contained in the Athanasian anathemas. There are many severe sentences in Scripture. But there is none which says even of murderers or of hypocrites, '*Whosoever* is a murderer, *whosoever* is a hypocrite, '*shall without doubt perish everlastingly*'—or, ' This ' and this is the exact scheme of Christian morality, ' which, *unless any one do keep whole and undefiled he* ' *cannot be saved.*' Qualifications, hopes, reservations not only come in, of necessity, from the nature of the subject-matter, but in fact prevent the utterance of such universal and misleading statements. But, in regard to opinions, declarations of this kind cannot fail to assume a more precise and direct meaning, because, if they have any force at all, they attack the opinions as in themselves fatal.

It is quite true that persons may think that they hold this or that opinion, when they are in fact holding its opposite; and that opinions are more or less valuable, more or less culpable, according to the amount of thought and care with which they are formed. But this is to substitute another proposition

_{Encouragement of party and personal animosities against individuals.}

altogether. If this be what is meant, then it is not opinions, as such, which are condemned, but certain moral qualities, such as negligence or idleness, which are not mentioned in the Creed at all. Or again, to speak of them as applying only to those 'who wilfully 'reject the truth' is, as we shall presently show, either supposing a case which never can occur, or is directing them against cases for which they would be universally felt to be far too strong. The nearest approach to such a state of mind that can be conceived is that of persons who, believing a certain statement to be true or false, afterwards, on the authority of some imaginary oracle (as of the Pope, or the like), or from some worldly motive, renounce their former convictions. Yet even here the severest critic would not say of every one who having announced a certain dogma to be false yet afterwards accepts it, that he 'shall without doubt perish ever-'lastingly.' In point of fact, no one ever does venture so to speak even of these extreme cases. No one would venture to say it of Cranmer after his recantations, nor of those unfortunate Roman Catholics who, after having asserted the Pope's fallibility, are now by weight of influence or authority constrained to assert the reverse. By the growth of this more Christian feeling the damnatory clauses have, therefore, been removed as much as possible into the innocuous sphere of general statements, as unlike as possible to the stringency and force with which they were in-

tended to attack 'whosoever does not hold the Catholic
'Faith whole and undefiled.' And wherever a strong
reason exists to exclude any particular class from
their operation, as is the case at present in regard to
the feeling of English High Churchmen towards the
Eastern Church, every nerve is strained to evacuate
their significance. So, again, no one thinks of applying them to those vast numbers of innocent English
men, women, and children who, by their necessary
misapprehension of the terms of the Athanasian
Creed, fall into the very errors which it denounces.

But although this system of reservations implies a
general disbelief in the damnatory clauses, they do,
nevertheless, not only retain, by the very force and
plainness of their language, their own hard, fast line,
but, in fact, are still kept, 'like sleeping lions to be
'rattled up' when there is occasion to bring them into
play against particular classes or individuals to whom
a special animosity may be felt. The modern Unitarian has but little really in common with the old
Alexandrian Arius. The modern philosophic theologian has but little in common with the old African
Sabellius. But the names of Arian and Sabellian still
linger, and whoever is connected by party warfare with
one or other of those ill-fated titles, is in such party
warfare brought within the condemnation of the Creed.
Contrary to all history and all scripture, those clauses
foster the notion that exact statements respecting the
Three Hypostases are more important than exact

statements respecting the moral nature of God, or the character of Christ, or the love of truth, or the necessity of toleration, or the supremacy of conscience. Therefore it has been thought not presumptuous to declare that Sabellians would in the other world 'be 'in quite a different condition from those who are not 'Sabellians.' Therefore an expectation, almost a hope, has been expressed, that a frightful, sudden death, such as that which befell Arius in the streets of Constantinople, would be inflicted on an eminent scholar who had come to take his part in making better understood the Holy Scriptures, and in kneeling with his brethren round the table of their common Lord, because he was supposed to hold the opinions of Milton, of Sir Isaac Newton, and of Channing.

Sentiments like these are difficult to reconcile with the principles involved in the honour paid to the good Samaritan, and the heathen soldier, and the Canaanite woman, and the man who cast out devils without following with the disciples. But they are the natural fruits of the ancient damnatory clauses, and of the damnatory spirit of the age whence those clauses originated. The meaning of the clauses is now reduced, by 'considerable intellectual caution,' to something much more like the spirit of the Gospel. But, to anyone who accepts them in their full sense, or who is influenced by their original intention, it is only natural that the persons against whom they are believed to be directed should be viewed with unspeakable horror. A man, of whom we are unhesitatingly able to say that, '*he shall, without doubt, perish ever-'lastingly*,' must be the most miserable of human beings—to be avoided, not only in sacred, but in common intercourse, as something too awful to be approached or spoken of.

V. It is not necessary to say more than a few words in reference to the professions of warm attachment to this Creed which at various times have been made. It is evident that Waterland defends the Creed only on condition that its language may not be accepted literally and in detail. Of Dr. Donaldson's vindication of the Creed we have already spoken. Dr. Newman, in his 'Grammar of Assent,' has uttered an impassioned eulogy upon it; but it must be remembered that in the same work he refers to it, without question, as the composition of St. Athanasius; that he cites, without indication of its spuriousness, the apocryphal verse of 1 John v. 7; that he treats as an open question the popular notion of endless punishment which it is believed to endorse; and, as we have seen, has elsewhere declared that he attaches no meaning to one of its most important theological phrases. A recent exposition confines the application of its curses to the educated; but from them requires an absolute assent, —that is to say, in proportion to the carefulness and learning with which the enquirer may have arrived at an opposite conclusion.

It may, however, be worth while to treat at greater

<small>Its interpretations.</small>

length an interpretation which doubtless commends itself more readily, not only because of the far higher authority from which it comes, but also because it has a basis of truth, which in the other explanations is almost entirely wanting;[1] and because, if rightly understood, it will possibly reconcile those who adopt it more easily to acquiesce in any proposed change. We do not mean by this merely the fact that the revered author of that interpretation, with his usual candour, expresses his conviction 'that it is impossible 'much longer to retain the Athanasian Creed as part 'of our services, and that if a composition so weighty 'and awful, treating of the most transcendent topics 'in the most distinct language, requires explanations 'and compromises which destroy reverence and intro-'duce confusion, its worth for our common worship 'must be gone.' It is more important to observe that the interpretation itself is such as more than establishes the conclusions at which its excellent expounder has arrived; that 'just because one honours 'it and has learnt deep lessons from it, one must 'desire that it should not be heard in public, that it 'should be kept only for secret meditation.'

This principle of interpretation rests on the ground that by tracing the ideas of the Creed behind its out-

[1] See *A Few More Words on the Athanasian Creed*, by Professor Maurice, in the October number of the *Contemporary Review*. Some ingenious arguments to the same effect may be found (on the words—'keep the faith,' 'saved,' 'perish') in Mr. Swainson's treatise on *The Athanasian Creed*, pp. 50-61.

ward form into the inner source from which they
spring, and by tracing back the meaning of its words
as they occur in the Creed to the meaning which they
have in the Bible (so far as they occur there at all)
—a true and valuable sense may be found both for
its dogmatical statements and for its condemnatory
clauses. The sense which is thus found for the Creed
is far more spiritual and exalted than that ascribed
to it by its usual advocates. This interpretation is
thus the most favourable specimen of the endeavour to affix to an ancient document a meaning
different from its ordinary, and, as far as we know
anything of the matter, its historical sense; and it
may be useful to take the occasion of pointing out
that the like process might be applied to almost every
serious document ever put forward by any Church in
Christendom, and that in spite of any such possible
interpretation such documents have nevertheless been
discarded as unfit for public use.

Explanation by reducing the phrases to their original meaning in the Bible.

1. We would take two examples. One is 'the
'Solemn League and Covenant.' Whatever may be
said of the original adoption of the Athanasian Creed
by the French or Spanish Church, it can hardly be
said at any time to have been consciously adopted as
the expression of the faith of the English nation. But
the Solemn League and Covenant may truly claim
the credit of having, alone of all British Creeds,
the deliberate assent of the whole Legislature, and
the ardent welcome of the whole kingdom. Its very

Parallel case of the Solemn League and Covenant.

title is a history of the profound conviction and general acceptance with which it was adopted. It is 'the 'Solemn League and Covenant for Reformation and 'Defence of Religion, the Honour and Happiness of 'the King, and the Peace and Safety of the Three 'Kingdoms of Scotland, England, and Ireland; agreed 'upon by Commissioners from the Parliament and 'Assembly of Divines in England, with Commis-'sioners of the Convention of Estates, and General 'Assembly in Scotland; approved by the General 'Assembly of the Church of Scotland, and by both 'Houses of Parliament and Assembly of Divines in 'England, and taken and subscribed by them, *Anno* '1643; and thereafter, by the said authority, taken 'and subscribed by all Ranks in Scotland the same 'Year; and ratified by Act of the Parliament of 'Scotland, *Anno* 1644: And again renewed in Scot-'land, with an Acknowledgment of Sins, and Engage-'ment to Duties, by all Ranks, *Anno* 1648, and by 'Parliament 1649; and taken and subscribed by King 'Charles II. at Spey, June 23, 1650; and at Scoon, 'January 1, 1651.' No other Confession of Faith in any time of our ecclesiastical history—certainly not the Thirty-nine Articles, still less 'the Creed of St. 'Athanasius'—has been accepted with such an overwhelming weight of moral enthusiasm, as that which was exhibited when the Solemn League and Covenant was signed with tears and blood in the Greyfriars' Church at Edinburgh, or when it was read to both

Houses of Parliament and to the Assembly of Divines from the pulpit of St. Margaret's Church in Westminster, 'with an audible voice article by article, each 'person standing uncovered, with his right hand lifted 'up bare to heaven, worshipping the great name of 'God, and swearing to the performance of it.' And most assuredly it would be as easy in its case, as in the case of the Athanasian Creed, to discover a true Biblical sense in the sacred words which it uses, and a Christian significance which may be wrapped up in its strange statements and bitter denunciations. Its damnatory clauses are almost as dogmatic and almost as unsparing as the Athanasian anathemas. Its subscribers are pledged to 'the extirpation of 'Popery, Prelacy (that is, church-government by 'Archbishops, Bishops, their Chancellors and Com-'missaries, Deans, Deans and Chapters, Archdeacons, 'and all other ecclesiastical Officers depending on 'that hierarchy), superstition, heresy, schism, profane-'ness, and whatsoever shall be found to be contrary 'to sound doctrine and the power of godliness, lest 'we partake in other men's sins, and thereby be in 'danger to receive of their plagues: and that the 'Lord may be one, and his name one, in the three 'kingdoms;' to the 'discovery of all such as have 'been or shall be incendiaries, malignants, or evil 'instruments, by hindering the reformation of religion, 'dividing the king from his people, or one of the 'kingdoms from another, or making any faction or

'parties among the people, contrary to this League
'and Covenant; that they may be brought to public
'trial, and receive condign punishment, as the degree
'of their offences shall require or deserve, or the
'supreme judicatories of both kingdoms respectively,
'or others having power from them for that effect,
'shall judge convenient;' and to 'the securing and
'preserving the purity of religion against all error,
'heresy, and schism, and namely, Independency,
'Antinomianism, Arminianism, and Socinianism,
'Familism, Libertinism, Scepticism, and Erastian-
'ism.' No doubt here (as possibly in the Athanasian
Creed) there may have been a ground in the circumstances of the time, or in the nature of the opinions
and things denounced, for the fierceness of these
denunciations. No doubt, even at the time, qualifying
statements and 'explanatory notes' were adopted by
those who signed it. 'The word "League" was put
'into the title by Sir Harry Vane, as thinking that it
'might be broken sooner than "a Covenant," and in
'the first article he inserted that general phrase of
'reforming "according to the Word of God." When
'Mr. Coleman read the Covenant before the House of
'Lords in order to their receiving it, he declared that
'by "prelacy" *all* sorts of Episcopacy were not
'intended, but only the forms therein described. Thus
'the wise men on both sides endeavoured to outwit
'each other in wording the articles.'[1] A whole cata-

[1] Neal's *Puritans*, iii. 58–62, 370; Stoughton's *Church of the Civil Wars*, i. 324.

logue of 'salvos' were drawn up, by which those who were discontented with it might 'take it in their 'own sense.' And, in fact, most of 'the episcopal 'divines who made the greatest figure in the Church 'after the Restoration did not refuse it;' nor did the gay Charles II., nor did the chivalrous Montrose, nor the politic Elector Palatine, nor the holy Leighton. All ministers, old and young—noblemen, gentlemen, common councilmen, officers in the army—all pressed or were constrained to take it. One voice from amongst the dominant party resisted the general enthusiasm or the general compulsion. It was the same voice that afterwards was raised against the damnatory clauses of the Athanasian Creed. 'Mr. 'Baxter,' we are told, 'kept his people from taking 'the Covenant lest it should be a snare to them.'[1] It is evident that whatever explanations are applicable to the Athanasian clauses would, if it were still in use amongst us, be applicable to the Covenant. A staunch Episcopalian could have used the denunciations against Episcopacy with a similar 'Explanatory Note' to that which enables a charitable or enquiring divine to use the Athanasian Creed. And had it seemed good to the Church of England or to the Church of Scotland (as it has still seemed good to that small section of the Church of Scotland which prides itself on being the only true representative of that body) to preserve and recite this document amongst its standards of

[1] Neal's *Puritans*, 7.

faith, a devout and philosophical Churchman might have found reasons for doing so, as now for the Athanasian Creed.

Yet, in spite of these reasons for retaining this solemn Confession, thus grandly inaugurated, it has, in the Church of England, been suppressed altogether, and in the Church of Scotland been reduced to that condition in which the Athanasian Creed, according to the proposal of a distinguished living prelate, ought to be reduced in the Church of England, namely, relegated to the close of its authorised formularies, without any binding obligation for its general use. One only echo remains of that which was once the voice of the United Church of Great Britain. The sect of the Cameronians, or, as they call themselves, 'the ' Reformed Presbyterian Church of Scotland,' still subscribe and still recite the Solemn League and Covenant. In the north of Ireland, where they are cut off from the more civilising influences of the mother-country, they rehearse the articles of this dogmatic Confession with all its damnatory clauses in their full original strength, and with their most direct application to those whom it denounced. Every celebration of their Communion is ushered in by the solemn recital of the Covenant, with a distinct and separate excommunication, first of the Queen and of all the Royal Family, and then of the several Churches of England and Scotland, Established and Free alike, as breakers of the Covenant. In the small remnant which lingers in Scotland the strength of the denunciations which invoke 'condign punishment on all 'malignants' is somewhat explained away. But with these qualifications, like to those which even the most rigid advocates of the Athanasian anathemas adopt in regard to the Greek Church, the Solemn League and Covenant still drags on an obscure and innocent existence—an exact sample probably of the manner in which 'the Creed of St. Athanasius' would be kept up in a few congregations, after it has been dropped in the nation at large by an assent as general as that which has consigned to oblivion the Creed of Henderson and Philip Nye, of Charles II., Montrose, and Leighton.

2. Another case shall be cited, which, perhaps, may come nearer home. From the year 1662 till the year 1859, three services, drawn up and authorised by Convocation, were ordered by the Privy Council to be read in churches on the 5th of November, the 30th of January, and the 29th of May. These services contained, after the manner (*mutatis mutandis*) of the Athanasian Creed and the Solemn League and Covenant, severe denunciations against the 'cruel, bloody, 'and violent men,' 'the malicious conspiracies and 'wicked practices' whereby the Long Parliament and the founders of the Commonwealth were supposed to carry on their designs in the Civil Wars, and 'against the secret contrivances and hellish 'malice,' 'the cruel and bloodthirsty enemies,' that

Parallel case of th Political Services.

were concerned in overthrowing the liberties of England in the reigns of the first and the second James. These services, until the time of their abolition, were, by many good men, as highly prized as the Athanasian Creed is now.[1] As the Athanasian Creed is made the subject of a well-known poem in the *Lyra Apostolica*, so those services are made the subjects of three, not the least beautiful, poems in the *Christian Year*. Many excellent men clung to them with a tenacity exactly similar to that now shown towards the *Quicunque Vult*,—sometimes from a mere fear of change, sometimes from a belief that they embodied important doctrines, sometimes from a genuine admiration, as the case might be, for the character of Charles I. or of William III. Time after time, when the question was raised in Convocation or elsewhere for their removal, as unsuited for public worship, it was met by determined opposition or quiet resistance. Here, as in the case of the Athanasian Creed, it was not difficult to find excuses for retaining them. The fierce feeling which breathed through them, however distasteful its expression to the large mass of Churchmen, must yet, by all candid men, be acknowledged

[1] It should be observed that one circumstance, which does not apply to the Athanasian Creed, somewhat broke the unanimity of the High Church party in regard to the Political Services. Sincerely attached as they were to the Services for the Martyrdom of Charles I. and the Restoration of Charles II., they had always a secret repugnance to the commemoration of the Revolution of 1688, in the Service of the 5th of November.

to have had some ground in the vehemence of resentment excused, if not justified, by the sacredness of the cause, whether of hereditary monarchy or of constitutional and religious liberty, which those services commemorated. Qualifications similar to those which are offered of the damnatory clauses consigning to everlasting perdition those who confound the Persons or deny the Double Procession, might be applied to the savage denunciations which these services launched respectively against the Puritans and the Roman Catholics. As it may be argued that the Athanasian curses, in truth, smite those whom their advocates intend to spare, and pass over those whom their advocates intend to condemn, so here Puritans might fairly argue that the description of Cromwell and Milton, as 'cruel men,' 'sons of Belial,' in the services of the 30th of January and the 29th of May, was, at least, equally applicable to the Cavaliers who advocated 'killing no murder;' and Jacobites might plead that the description of 'secret conspiracies' in the service of the 5th of November, could be used as a description of the Rye House Plot, no less than of the Gunpowder Plot; and of the invitation to the Prince of Orange, no less than of the machinations of James II.

Yet in spite of the arguments for retaining these interesting historical services, they excited generally the same kind of antipathy as the Athanasian Creed. Like the Athanasian Creed (till within the last forty years), they lingered only in college chapels or cathedrals, and from time to time the aversion to them made itself heard in the protests of individuals. Arnold more than once agitated for their removal. Dean Milman, on the few occasions in which he appeared in Convocation, in vain endeavoured to induce his brethren to take some steps for the abolition of so grievous a scandal. Another ecclesiastic, who has always advocated no less eagerly the relaxation of the use of the Athanasian Creed, made a point, on every 30th of January for several years, to write to the newspapers calling attention to the needless continuance of these emblems of extinct political controversy. Lord Ebury has more than once called the attention of the Legislature to them amongst other blots in the Liturgy. At last their hour came. The same distinguished nobleman who has taken a chief part in the conflict of the last two years in endeavouring to remove the stumbling-block of the Athanasian Creed, succeeded by a like union of conciliation and perseverance in removing from the Prayer-book the blot which, next to that Confession, was the one most keenly felt by the true friends of the Church of England. In 1858, Earl Stanhope moved in the House of Lords an address to the Queen for the withdrawal of the Order in Council which had hitherto enjoined the use of these ecclesiastical war-cries, and the two Houses of Parliament gladly concurred[1] in removing the indirect sanction

[1] The three services most inaccurately called 'State services,' had

which the celebration of this ancient party rancour had received from the Legislature. In those days, happily, the notion that every Act for the amelioration of the Church must pass through the intricate ordeal of the four houses of Convocation, had not occurred either to the Government or the clergy; and accordingly it came to pass that these services, which alone of all the services of the English Church had been drawn up and sanctioned almost exclusively by Convocation, and which had been protected by Convocation to the last, were withdrawn from public use, without the slightest reference to the Convocations either of Canterbury or York, and, it may be added, without the slightest murmur from those venerable bodies, at this contumelious rejection of their work, and absolute indifference to their claims. Here and there a solitary lament arose at the loss of what was deemed a national recognition of past mercies. A respected Professor of Divinity from Oxford lifted up a warning voice against the removal of this time-honoured landmark, as doubtless he would again, in

never received the sanction of Parliament, either during their composition or afterwards. Parliament had only enjoined that the days should be kept holy, but without specifying in what manner. The services themselves were strictly 'Convocation services.' The two for January 30 and May 29, were compiled, and that for the 5th of November revised, by Convocation in 1662; and though they were appended to the Common Prayer-book, and sanctioned (with some very slight subsequent alterations) by Orders in Council, they never received the sanction of the State in Parliament, and were, therefore, emphatically 'Church 'services' in the most limited sense.

the case of the removal of the Athanasian Creed. But, as a general rule, the three services have passed away without leaving a scar behind; and there is probably not a single clergyman throughout the country who would not now regret to see them restored. So will it always be with religious services which are the expression of sentiments that have ceased to live, and which are therefore only kept up as badges and symbols either of party strife, or of some idea which, however much it may be found by ingenious or charitable minds beneath their surface, does not obviously belong to them, and therefore cannot be pleaded for their retention.

It can hardly be urged that the attachment felt towards the Athanasian Creed is of a wider range or of a deeper root, than that formerly shown towards the Solemn League and Covenant or even the service for the 30th of January. But it is by seeing how the arguments used in favour of the Athanasian Creed may be equally used in favour of other documents of a totally different character, that we are best able to appreciate their futility at least for practical purposes. And the entire disappearance of the Solemn League and Covenant from the formularies of the Church of England, and its almost entire disappearance from those of the Church of Scotland; the removal of the services for the Political Anniversaries, although touching Convocation in its tenderest point, are samples of the mode in which, when the proper time arrives, ecclesiastical documents which have been the very apple of the eye to eager theological disputants may be laid to sleep for ever by anyone who has the courage to try the experiment.

VI. Amongst the judgments pronounced on the Athanasian Creed, the most deliberate ever given is that delivered by the Royal Commissioners appointed in 1867 'to enquire into the Rubrics, Orders, ' and directions for regulating the course and conduct ' of the public worship of the Church of England.' Judgment of the Ritual Commission.

Of the twenty-seven Commissioners who have signed the Report, a small minority have been content to leave unaltered the rubric enforcing the use of the Creed, but on the condition of adding an explanatory note. The history of this explanatory note is given in the Minutes. A considerable effort had been made to resist the discussion of the Rubric enjoining the use of the Creed, not on its own merits, but on the ground that it was beyond the scope of the Commission. This was at last overruled. (Minutes, pp. 83, 84, 86, 102.) Then, after various ineffectual attempts to procure the relaxation or omission of the Rubric (pp. 102, 118), it was at last proposed that 'the Epis- ' copal members of the Commission be requested to ' prepare an explanatory note for the consideration of ' the Commissioners.' (Minutes, p. 118.) The explanatory note.

The note as proposed by those Bishops who were willing to undertake the task was as follows :— First note

That no words in this Creed are to be understood as pronouncing sentence of eternal condemnation on those who do not hold every one of its separate propositions, or through involuntary ignorance, even the Catholic Faith itself, but as solemnly warning of their peril those who having been called into a state of salvation wilfully renounce the Catholic Faith.

This note was, after discussion, withdrawn. (Minutes, p. 122.)

Second note.

Another form of note suggested by another Bishop was as follows :—

Although this confession of our Christian Faith ought, without doubt, to be received as being warranted by Holy Scripture, yet for the avoidance of all scruple in the use thereof, be it noted :

1. That the words the Holy Ghost is of the Father and the Son, not made, nor created, nor begotten, but proceeding, do not declare the Holy Ghost to proceed from the Son so as in any wise to contradict the Catholic doctrine that the Father alone is the fountain head of the Triune Godhead.

2. That the clauses which declare the necessity of a right belief to eternal salvation are not to be understood as excluding from salvation those who through involuntary ignorance or misapprehension do not receive aright the Truth of God, but those only who through a perverse will reject it in whole or in part.

This note was withdrawn without discussion. (Minutes, p. 122.)

Third note.

A third form of note was then proposed to the following effect :—

The condemnations in this Confession of Faith are to be

JUDGMENT OF THE RITUAL COMMISSION. 75

no otherwise understood than as a solemn warning of the peril of those who wilfully reject the Catholic Faith.

This note was carried by eleven to seven. Of those eleven, two have since disclaimed the note, and two have declined to sign any part of the Report. The adherents of this course therefore at the time of the publication of the Report were reduced to seven, and are now probably fewer still. Adopted by seven.

On the other hand,[1] nineteen of the Commissioners have expressed their desire, in terms more or less direct, that the Creed shall cease to be enforced in public worship. Condemnatio of the use of the Creed by the majority of the Commissioner

1. The ARCHBISHOP OF CANTERBURY :—

Respecting the Athanasian Creed, while I rejoice that the Commissioners have thought it right to append a Rubric explanatory of the sense in which 'the condemnations in ' this Confession of Faith' are to be understood, I cannot feel entirely satisfied with this course.

The adoption by the Commissioners of this explanation seems to me to admit two things,—

1st. That it was within the power of the Commission to deal with the use of the Athanasian Creed :

2nd. That the use of the Creed in public worship was liable, from the wording of those clauses, to objection.

---

[1] The reason of the apparent contradiction between what is called in the Report the decision of 'the Commission,' and that which in fact is the decision of the majority of the Commission, is easily explained. The decision of 'the Commission' was made in a meeting in which the real majority of the Commissioners were absent, from illness and other causes, and had therefore not the opportunity of expressing their dissent till after the completion of the Report framed by what was in fact a small minority of their body.

I should, therefore, have deemed it a wiser course had the Commission decided that the Creed in question, valuable and most important as are its direct doctrinal statements, should not retain its place in the Public Service of the Church. (Report, p. viii.)

2. EARL STANHOPE:—

In the course of our deliberations the propriety of retaining the Athanasian Creed in the public Services was frequently discussed, the objection being felt more especially as regards its so-called damnatory clauses. It seemed to very many among us that these clauses are both a blemish in our beautiful Liturgy and a danger to our national Church. However they may be explained to the satisfaction of learned men conversant with the terms of scholastic divinity in the Greek and Latin languages, it is certain that they are a stumbling-block to common congregations; forming a service which is wholly misunderstood by some persons, and in which it is observed that others decline to join.

Various proposals were made in our body to meet the general and growing objections which these clauses in the Athanasian Creed, and consequently on them the entire Creed, have raised. It was moved that in the preceding Rubric the word 'shall' should be changed to 'may.' It was moved to omit the preceding Rubric by which the use of that Creed is prescribed. It was moved to limit the use of that Creed, and that permissive only, to our public Services in collegiate and cathedral churches. It was moved to enjoin it for only one Sunday in the year. To several of us it would have appeared a still preferable plan, which, however, was not formally brought forward, to declare in a new Rubric that although the Church retained this Creed as a confession of our Christian faith, the Church did not enjoin its use in any of its public Services.

JUDGMENT OF THE RITUAL COMMISSION. 77

It was found, however, upon divisions, several of which took place at divers times in the course of our proceedings, that no one specific proposal could commend itself to the approval of a majority among us. We have, therefore, left untouched and without any suggestion for discontinuance in the appointed Services a Creed which, nevertheless, so far as regards its popular effect upon others, I imagine that scarce any Churchman contemplates with entire satisfaction. Nor am I at all satisfied with the note which our Report proposes to subjoin. Under these circumstances, which I most deeply regret, I altogether dissent from the very anomalous state in which, to my judgment, this question has been left. (Report, p. viii. ix.)

3. LORD PORTMAN :—

I concur in the opinions above expressed. (Report, p. ix.)

4. The EARL OF HARROWBY :—

I assent to the statement of facts in regard to the Athanasian Creed put forward by Lord Stanhope, and agree generally with the opinions he has expressed.

I only disagree so far, as that I do not dissent from the conclusions come to by the Commission.

In spite of the objections which I entertain to the language of certain clauses of the so-called Athanasian Creed, and to its use in public congregations, I have felt it my duty to concur with the majority of the Commission in retaining it as it now stands in the Prayer-book, on the ground that it seemed to me to be beyond the purpose of our Commission to remove a Confession of Faith from the position of authority, in which our Church has hitherto placed it. (Report, p. ix.)

5. The BISHOP OF WINCHESTER :—

I am not satisfied with the explanatory note appended to the Athanasian Creed. (Report, p. x.)

The same Prelate also 'called attention to the 'question of placing the Creed with the Articles of 'Religion at the end of the Book of Common Prayer.' (See Report, p. 106.)

6. The BISHOP OF ST. DAVID'S:—

I protest against the compulsory use of the Athanasian Creed, as not only an evil, on acount of the effect it produces on many of the most intelligent and attached members of our Church, but a wrong in itself. It may be impossible to ascertain the extent of the evil, or the proportion of those who are offended by the Creed, to those who acquiesce in it, or even find themselves edified by it. But this appears to me a point of comparatively little moment. The important question is, whether those who are offended by the Creed have just and reasonable ground of objection to it. I think they have. It appears to me that, in adopting such a document, the Church both overstept the bounds of its rightful authority, and exercised the usurped authority in an uncharitable and mischievous way. Nothing, as it seems to me, could have warranted such a step, but a special revelation, placing the Creed on a level with Holy Writ. It may be possible for Theologians to show, by technical arguments, that it is a legitimate development of doctrine implicitly contained in Scripture. But this, however fully admitted, would not justify the Church in exacting assent to their conclusions under the penalty of eternal perdition. This was in fact creating a new offence against the Divine Law, and introducing a new term of salvation, on merely human authority. Looking to the period when this innovation was first imposed on Christians, we may find much excuse for its authors. But viewed in the light of the fundamental principles of a Reformed Church, it appears to me, as forming part of our public services, utterly indefensible.

JUDGMENT OF THE RITUAL COMMISSION. 79

I strongly disapprove of the Explanatory Note which has been appended to the Athanasian Creed. I believe not only that it must fail to serve the purpose for which it was adopted, but that it will aggravate the evil it was designed to remedy. If the 'condemnations' have hitherto been generally misunderstood—which I do not believe to be the case—it is too late for any Commission, even if it could speak with authority, to correct the error of public opinion on this head; and if this was possible, it could not be effected by an explanation which is vitiated by the ambiguity of the term 'wilfully,' on which the whole meaning depends. The unsuccessful attempt will I believe be generally regarded as the admission of an evil, which ought to have been treated in a different manner, or left untouched. (Report, p. xi.)

7. LORD EBURY 'desires to concur in the above 'protest.' (Report, p. xi.)

8. MR. JOHN ABEL SMITH, M.P., 'desires to concur 'in the above protest.' (Report, p. xi.)

9. The BISHOP OF CARLISLE :—

With regard to the Athanasian Creed.—It may be doubted whether the consideration of this subject was within the limits of your Majesty's Commission; but the Commissioners having determined so to regard it, I regret that it was not found possible to arrive at a more satisfactory solution of the difficulty which many persons feel, than the addition of a note, which, I venture to think, is incomplete as an explanation, and insufficient to meet the scruples of those who object to the public recitation of this Confession of our Christian Faith. (Report, p. xiii.)

The same Prelate proposed that the use of the Creed should be prohibited in parish churches, but permitted, though not enforced, in cathedral and collegiate churches. (See Minutes, p. 228.)

10. The RIGHT HON. SPENCER H. WALPOLE:—

The note appended to this Creed or Confession of Faith furnishes to my mind the strongest proof that, however valuable such a document may be as an historical exposition of the Church's views, the enforced use of it as a symbol of faith in Public Worship is most unadvisable. It seems to me to be very objectionable that a congregation should be required to affirm and profess the articles of their Creed in language which obviously and in its natural sense means one thing, when the interpretation put upon it says that it means another. (Report, p. xiii.)

11. The RIGHT HON. SIR JOSEPH NAPIER:—

With reference to the annotation proposed to be made in explanation of the penal clauses of the Creed commonly known as the Athanasian Creed, I humbly submit that we were not authorised by your Majesty to suggest any alteration in this or any other part of the services set forth in the Book of Common Prayer, and least of all by the imposition of a meaning of which the words are not susceptible. (Report, p. xiii.)

12. SIR TRAVERS TWISS, THE QUEEN'S ADVOCATE:—

I humbly submit to your Majesty, that evidence has been given before your Majesty's Commissioners, that this Confession of Faith is in practice disused by many of the Clergy, partly from personal repugnance to its language, partly from deference to the repugnance of their Congregations. Petitions have also been addressed to the President of Your Majesty's Commission from Clergy praying for relief, as regards the use of this Confession of Faith. Under these circumstances, if the occasional use of this Confession of Faith is still to be sanctioned, it seems to me that it would be in accordance with the spirit of your Majesty's instructions, that the Rubric, by which its use is made imperative on certain Festivals, should be modified. I consider it to be beyond the province of your Majesty's Commissioners to interpret the language of this Confession of Faith, and to put a construction, as proposed, by authority upon the so-called damnatory clauses, which is at variance with their plain and grammatical sense. (Report, p. xiv.)

13. MR. CHARLES BUXTON, M.P.:—

I desire humbly to express to your Majesty my deep regret that the Royal Commission has not recommended such changes in the Rubric before the so-called Athanasian Creed as could have put an end to its use as part of the Services of the Church of England; because—

(1) It seems to me that there is great presumption in the attempt made by that Creed to give a precise definition of the nature of the Supreme Being;

(2) The assertions it makes as to the nature of the Supreme Being are nowhere to be found stated in such terms in Holy Writ: but they are the deductions drawn from Scripture by the theologians of the period in which it was written. Now I cannot think that a Christian Creed ought to consist of inferences (however logical) drawn from Scripture, but only (like the Apostles' Creed) of the very statement of Scripture itself, given in its own words.

(3) Its declaration, that those who do not accept its statement of the Christian Faith, without doubt

will perish everlastingly, is generally acknowledged to be false, and nothing can be less fitting than to invite the people to make a solemn asseveration of that which it is not even wished that they should believe.

(4) It commits the Church of England to the doctrine, long since exploded, that error is a crime, punishable with horrible torments.

I object to the Note that it is proposed to append to the Athanasian Creed, because, in my opinion, it affirms that which is clearly contrary to the fact. The Athanasian Creed was written at a time when all men firmly believed that erroneous doctrine would be punished with everlasting perdition; and it was undoubtedly intended as a denunciation of such perdition against all those who did not hold that statement of doctrine which it sets forth. Accordingly, it precedes the statement by the words, 'which faith except ' every one do keep whole and undefiled, without doubt he ' shall perish everlastingly; and the Catholic Faith is this,' —it concludes the statement by saying, ' This is the Catholic ' Faith, which except a man believe faithfully he cannot be ' saved.' The meaning of this declaration at the beginning and ending of its statement of the Catholic Faith does not surely admit of any doubt whatever. Were there any such doubt, it would be altogether extinguished by the additional words thrown into the middle of the Creed. ' He therefore ' that will be saved must thus think of the Trinity. Further- ' more it is necessary to everlasting salvation that he also ' believe rightly.' . . . . . I consider, therefore, that it is only by perverting the obvious meaning of the above words, that we can aver, in the language of the Note, that they ' are to be no otherwise understood than as a solemn warn- ' ing of the peril of those who *wilfully* reject the Catholic ' Faith.' (Report, p. xvi.)

14. The DEAN OF WESTMINSTER :—

I desire to express my conviction that it was the duty of those who served on Your Majesty's Commission to recommend the relaxation of the use of the Athanasian Creed in the service of the Church of England. This might have been effected either by the substitution of 'may' for 'shall' in the Rubric, or by the omission of the Rubric altogether, according to the two proposals of Lord Stanhope; or by forbidding its use in parish churches, whilst permitting but not enforcing it in cathedral and collegiate churches, according to the proposal of the Bishop of Carlisle; or by leaving it to be used alternately with the Apostles' Creed, according to the conditional proposal of Mr. Perry; or by 'calling 'attention to the question of placing it with the Articles of 'Religion, at the end of the Book of Common Prayer,' according to the proposal of the Bishop of Winchester. Any one of these recommendations would have relieved the consciences of those who are burdened by its use without depriving those who are attached to it of the advantage which may, in their judgment, be derived from the retention of the Creed in the formularies of the Church.

I deeply regret that a change, proposed with such evident endeavours to conciliate the scruples of those opposed to it, should have been rejected; and I beg to offer the following reasons for that regret:

1. Because the Creed was received and enforced in the Church of England when it was believed to be 'the Creed 'of St. Athanasius,' whereas it is now known to be the work of an unknown author, not earlier than the fifth century, perhaps as late as the eighth.

2. Because its exposition of the doctrine of the Trinity is couched in language extremely difficult to be understood by a general congregation, in parts absolutely certain to be understood in a sense different from what was intended by

the original words; as, for example, 'person,' 'substance,' and 'incomprehensible.'

3. Because it is never recited in a mixed congregation in any other Church than our own.

4. Because the parts of the Creed which are at once most emphatic, most clear, and most generally intelligible are the condemning clauses which give most offence, and which in their literal and obvious sense are rejected by the Explanatory Note which is now proposed to be appended to them.

5. Because the use of anathemas in the public services of all Churches has been generally discontinued.

6. Because these condemning clauses assert in the strongest terms a doctrine now rejected by the whole civilized world, viz. the certain future perdition of all who deviate from the particular statements in the Creed.

7. Because they directly exclude from salvation all members of the Eastern Churches; to whom, nevertheless, the clergy and the bishops of the Church of England, at various times, and especially of late, have made overtures of friendly and Christian intercourse, entirely inconsistent with the declaration that they 'shall without doubt perish everlast-' ingly.'

8. Because the passage commonly quoted from the Authorized Version of Mark xvi. 16, in their defence, is irrelevant; (*a*) as being much more general in its terms; (*b*) as being of very doubtful genuineness; (*c*) as being in the original Greek much less severe than in the English translation.

9. Because the use of this Creed, and of those clauses especially, has been condemned by some of the most illustrious divines of the Church of England, such as Chillingworth, Baxter, Bishop Jeremy Taylor, Archbishop Tillotson, Archbishop Secker, Dr. Hey, Dr. Arnold, Dr. Burton, Bishop Lonsdale.

10. Because the use of the Creed arouses scruples in candidates for ordination which can only be overcome by strained explanations.

11. Because it has been rejected by the Protestant Episcopal Church of the United States of America, which is in full communion with the Church of England, and whose clergy are authorized by statute to minister in our churches, being yet under no obligation to use this Creed.

12. Because it is a stumbling-block in the way of almost all Nonconformists.

13. Because the public use of the Creed as a confession of Christian Faith, being, as it is, the composition of an unknown author, and not confirmed by any general authority, is a manifest violation of the well-known decrees of the Councils of Ephesus and Chalcedon.

14. Because the recitation of the Creed had in many English Churches become obsolete, till it was revived some thirty years ago.

15. Because many excellent laymen, including King George III., have for the last hundred years at least, declined to take part in its recitation.

16. Because so far from recommending the doctrine of the Trinity to unwilling minds, it is the chief obstacle in the way of the acceptance of that doctrine.

For these reasons I consider that the relaxation of the use of the Creed, whilst giving relief to many, ought to offend none. It has, no doubt, a historical value as an exposition of the teaching and manners of the Church between the fifth and ninth centuries. It has also a theological value, as rectifying certain erroneous statements; and as excluding from the essentials of the Catholic Faith the larger part of modern controversy. But these advantages are quite insufficient to outweigh the objections which are recorded above, and which, even in the minds of those disposed to retain the use of the Creed, have found expression in an Explanatory Note, tantamount to a condemnation of it.

With regard to the Explanatory Note, whilst acknowledging the benefit derived from the indirect but unquestionable discouragement which it inflicts on the use of the Creed, I would humbly state the reasons why it appears to me to aggravate the mischief which it is intended to relieve.

1. Because it attempts a decision on a complex dogmatical and historical question which the Commission is not called to offer, and which it has not attempted in other instances, equally demanding and more capable of such explanations, such as the Baptismal Service, the Ordination Service, and the Visitation of the Sick.

2. Because this dogmatical decision was carried by a small majority in a Commission of reduced numbers; whereas in order to have any weight it ought to have received the general concurrence of those most qualified to pronounce it.

3. Because the words in the Creed which it professes to explain are perfectly clear in themselves, whilst it leaves unexplained other words, such as 'person,' 'substance,' 'incomprehensible,' which are popularly understood in a sense different from their original meaning, and which as so understood mislead the mass of the congregation and even preachers into some of the very opinions so terribly denounced by the condemning clauses.

4. Because the statement which it implies is historically false, viz. that 'the condemnations in this Confession of Faith' do not apply to the persons to whom they evidently were intended to apply.

5. Because the main statement which it contains is either extremely questionable or a mere truism, or else so ambiguous as to be only misleading.

6. Because, after well considering a similar explanation given in 1689, Archbishop Tillotson thus expressed himself:

—'The account given of Athanasius' Creed appears to me 'nowise satisfactory. I wish we were well rid of it.'

7. Because, in most instances, it will give no ease to those who are offended by the use of the Creed in public services.

8. Because, whilst virtually condemning the use of the Creed, it still leaves the Rubric enjoining that use.

9. Because it will have the effect of increasing the existing burden by seeming to state that in the view of the Commission it is a sufficient remedy.

10. Because it is one of several proposed explanatory notes which appear in the Minutes, and which are manifestly inconsistent with this and with each other.

11. Because (in the language used by our chairman,[1] in putting it to the vote), it is 'illogical and unsatisfactory.' (Report, pp. xvii. xviii.)

15. The DEAN OF LINCOLN (Regius Professor of Divinity at Cambridge):—

I am unable to recommend that the Rubric which prescribes the use of this Creed should be retained:

Because an Exposition of Faith, containing a series of subtle definitions on the most abstruse points of doctrine, may be fitly placed among the Articles of Religion, but is ill-adapted to be 'sung or said' in the public worship of the Church.

Because the condemning clauses which precede and follow those definitions, when understood in their obvious sense, cause extreme distress of mind to many men of unquestionable piety, who unfeignedly believe all the Articles of the Christian Faith.

Because, however desirable it may be to present an authoritative interpretation of the Creed, the Commission has no authority to interpret doctrinal statements; and the Note,

[1] The Bishop of Winchester.

which it is proposed to add, seems rather to attest the fact than to diminish the force of grave and serious objections.

Because the Church has omitted the anathematizing clauses at the end of the Nicene Creed, as it stood originally; and the principle thus applied to a Creed which was sanctioned by a General Council might, with at least equal propriety, be applied to a Creed which was composed at a later age, and by an unknown author.

Because the Protestant Episcopal Church of the United States of America, which has not only rejected the use of the Athanasian Creed, in its public services, but even omitted all reference to the Creed itself in the Eighth of the Articles of Religion, is not the less cordially acknowledged to be in full communion with the Church of England. (Report, p. xix.)

16. The REV. CANON PAYNE SMITH (Regius Professor of Divinity at Oxford) :—

I object to the Note appended to the Creed commonly but erroneously called the Creed of St. Athanasius, for the following reasons :

1. Because the Commission possessed neither the right nor the authority to put an interpretation upon any of the formularies of the Church.

2. Because the Note explains the anathemas of the Creed in a manner contrary to their plain grammatical sense, and thereby introduces into the Prayer Book the principle of the non-natural interpretation of the Creeds and Formularies of the Church; a principle fatal to the maintenance of any standard of doctrine whatsoever.

3. Because the Note gives no ease or relief to the consciences of those who are offended by the recitation of this Creed at Public Worship.

I venture further humbly to express my opinion that this

Creed ought not to be publicly recited in the Church, for the following reasons :

1. Because the recitation of a Creed so intolerant is contrary to the right spirit of public worship, as being destructive of that calm and reverent frame of mind in which men ought to approach God. The anathema appended to the Nicene Creed is by the general consent of the Church never recited at public worship.

2. Because the anathemas of the Athanasian Creed are not warranted by Holy Writ, exclude apparently the whole Eastern Church from the possibility of salvation, and require men to believe, under pain of perishing everlastingly, not merely the plain statements of Holy Scripture, but deductions gathered from it by human reasoning.

3. Because the recitation of this Creed is a violation of Church principles, and condemned in the severest terms by the highest ecclesiastical authority. For the Church of England professes to receive the four first General Councils as next in authority to Holy Scripture, and accordingly the bishops of the whole Anglican Communion at the recent Lambeth Conference affirmed that they received the faith as defined by these Councils. But the Council of Constantinople in its seventh Canon, and that of Chalcedon in the Definition of the Faith appended to its Acts, expressly forbid 'the composing, exhibiting, producing, or teaching of 'any other Creed.' For this they give a sufficient reason, namely, that the Nicene Creed as finally settled at Constantinople 'teaches completely the perfect doctrine con- 'cerning the Father, the Son, and the Holy Ghost, and fully 'explains the Incarnation of the Lord.' To guard more carefully against the imposition of new creeds they command that every bishop or clergyman so offending should be deposed, and every layman anathematized. It was only after long and patient deliberation that these Councils them-

selves made additions to the simpler Creed of the Primitive Church; and not merely is their sentence justly deserved, but the principles which guided them violated, when we are required to recite at public worship a highly complex and elaborate Creed, the statements of which have never been discussed at any Council or Synod of the Church, and which in so many particulars goes beyond the Definition of the Faith as settled in the four first General Councils.

As embodying, nevertheless, that particular explanation of the doctrine of the Trinity in Unity, gathered from Holy Scripture chiefly by the logical mind of St. Augustine, I think that this Creed ought by all means to be retained among the authoritative documents of the Church of England, mainly because of the general assent given to it by the whole Western Church; but only until such time as both its several clauses, and also the question of its general imposition in the face of the contrary decision of the Undivided Church, shall have been considered, if not by a General Council, at all events by a Synod representing all Christians in communion with the English Church. (Report, p. xx.)

17. The REV. HENRY VENN (Secretary of the Church Missionary Society) 'is unable to concur' in the retention of the existing Rubric and the Explanatory Note affixed to it. (Report, p. viii.)

18. The REV. W. G. HUMPHRY, Vicar of St. Martin's:—

I disapprove of the Note which has been appended to the Athanasian Creed in the Schedule, for the following reasons:

1. It is not within the province of the Commission to put an interpretation on one of the formularies of the Church.

2. The Note appears to me to put an interpretation on the

condemning clauses of the Creed which is at variance with their plain and obvious meaning. For according to the Note the condemnations of the Creed are intended only for those persons who '*wilfully reject* the Catholic Faith;' whereas the Creed declares that except every one do *keep* the Catholic Faith *whole and undefiled*, he cannot be saved; and again, 'This is the Catholic Faith, which except a man '*believe faithfully*, he cannot be saved.' The terms of condemnation, as expressed in the Creed, are manifestly far more comprehensive than the Note represents them to be.

3. It appears to me that the chief effect of the Note, if placed in the Prayer Book, will be to offend by an unsound explanation the consciences of many who at present acquiesce in the recitation of the Creed.

With regard to the recitation of the Creed in public worship, I concur generally in the opinions expressed by the Archbishop of Canterbury, the Bishop of St. David's, the Dean of Westminster, and Professor Payne Smith. (Report, p. xxi.)

19. The REV. T. W. PERRY:—

Having regard to the various and conflicting representations which were made to the Commissioners, they could not well avoid discussing the Rubric prefixed to the Athanasian Creed, although it cannot be pretended that any doubt exists as to its *meaning*, whatever may be thought of the fitness of the Rubric itself. But it appears to me that the terms of our Commission do not authorize us to make any recommendation to alter the prescribed use of this Creed, nor do I think they warrant our making a Note explanatory of the meaning of any part of the Creed. If there had been anything like a general unanimity of opinion among us as to the desirableness of some change in the Rubric, I think we might with some propriety have indicated that opinion, stating also that we were only precluded from making it a *recommendation* by the limitations which the Commission imposed upon us. It is true that in a very few instances we have altered Rubrics of whose meaning there is also no doubt, and so may have somewhat exceeded the strict letter of our Instructions : but these changes, while desired by some, are not likely to be objected to by others; whereas the serious opposition which would be made to any *recommendation* from us to put the Athanasian Creed in a position of inferiority to the other Creeds, could not but be materially strengthened by the knowledge that the Commissioners had thus transgressed their powers.

I do not consider it necessary to make any remarks upon the language of the Note itself, because it seems to me that no explanatory Note is likely to satisfy those who object to the use of this Creed in the Public Service of the Church ; but if it were desirable to furnish an explanation for the sake of others, I think the wording of this Note would need some alteration. (Report, p. xxiv.)

Mr. Perry proposed (under these circumstances) that permission should be given to use the Apostles' Creed instead of the 'Creed of St. Athanasius' on the appointed days. (See Minutes, p. 127.)

Such is the result of the most deliberate discussion which has ever taken place in the English Church on the Athanasian Creed. It is not too much to say that it amounts to a unanimous condemnation of the present use of the Creed.

Out of a body of twenty-seven the large majority, consisting of nineteen, have expressed their opinion,

JUDGMENT OF THE RITUAL COMMISSION. 93

with various degrees of force, that the use of the Creed should no longer be made obligatory. On the other side are a small minority, apparently of seven,[1] who are willing that the Creed should be continued if accompanied by an Explanatory Note. But that Note, whilst it has been condemned in strong terms by the large majority of the Commissioners, is an acknowledgment, even by the minority, that the Creed, in the sense in which it is ordinarily used, ought not to be read: 'How offensive, how extremely 'painful,' such an explanation must be to the more high-minded advocates of the Creed, it needed not the burning words of Professor Maurice to express.[2]

[1] As these seven Commissioners had not the opportunity of stating their reasons for their course, it seemed more respectful to them in this essay not to record their names.

[2] It may be worth while briefly to indicate the difference between Mr. Maurice's interpretation of the Creed, and that contained in the 'Explanatory Note' or other like qualifications. Mr. Maurice's principle is substantially that set forth in Mr. Wilson's able *Lectures on the Communion of Saints*, in which he lays down (in reference to that article of the Creed) that 'the sense of formularies founded on the 'Scriptures must be sought in the declarations and history of Scripture 'rightly understood, and interpreted according to the best lights of 'those who in each age are responsible for their judgment upon it' (p. 33); and it is obvious that this specially applies to cases where, as in the Athanasian Creed, the words used are actually taken from Scripture, such as 'salvation,' 'Father,' 'Son,' 'Holy Ghost,' and the quotation from Matt. xxv. 41, 46. The difficulty of applying this interpretation (over and above the general considerations suggested in the first part of this article) is, first, that several of the most important words in the Creed, such as 'substance,' 'person,' 'Trinity,' 'Catholic Faith,' 'uncreate,' 'conversion,' 'confusion,' either do not occur at all in Scripture, or occur only in senses so remote as to be hardly recog-

How useless to imagine that it will satisfy any scruples, or have any other effect than covering the Confession itself with contempt, has been set forth in the weighty sentences of the Bishop of St. David's.

One like example of explanation has been given of another like document. The recent dogma of the Pope's infallibility may, we are told, be accepted [1] with the explanation that the Pope is infallible because either we know that the moment he errs he *ipso facto* ceases to be Pope, or that as no Pope ever has spoken *ex cathedrâ* from the beginning of time till now, so it is probable that henceforth till the end of time none ever will so speak. The Athanasian clauses in like manner, we are told, only apply to those who 'wilfully reject the Catholic Faith.' It may safely be affirmed that in the only sense in which these words can have any meaning, no one ever did or ever

nisable; and, secondly, that those which do occur in Scripture are in the Creed so dislocated from their original context (except, perhaps, in the case of the quotation of Matt. xxv. 41, 46) as to make it inconceivable that to the author or the ordinary hearers of the Creed they should have conveyed their original meaning. Still, this mode of defending the Creed proceeds on a definite principle; and, of however little avail for practical exposition, has a legal and theological value which ought not to be lightly disparaged. But such an interpretation as that affixed on the Creed by the 'Explanatory Note' has no such justification. It is an alien and arbitrary sense attached to the words, almost avowedly in contradiction to their obvious meaning; and, moreover, pronounces a fresh judgment not contemplated in the Creed, and endeavours to explain what is in itself clear by a phrase so obscure and ambiguous as to introduce new elements of difficulty and deception.

[1] *What is the Meaning of the late Definition of the Infallibility of the Pope? An Enquiry.* By William Maskell, p. 10.

can 'wilfully reject the Catholic Faith.' Whether such interpretations are respectful to the documents which they profess to honour may well be doubted.

The unanimity of the decision is the more impressive from the variety of elements which have been brought to bear on the subject. Amongst the nineteen who have declared themselves against the present obligation to use the Creed, every one is represented. There is here no difference between Bishops and Presbyters. The two[1] Primates and the Bishop of Winchester appear on the same side of relaxation with the humblest parochial incumbent. Nor is it a question of political opinion. The Conservative legislators and lawyers, Earl Stanhope, Mr. Walpole, and Sir Joseph Napier, agree on this point with Lord Portman, Lord Ebury, Sir Travers Twiss, Mr. Buxton, and Mr. John Abel Smith. Nor is it a concord only of one ecclesiastical party. Not to speak of others, it is interesting to observe that, however wide their differences on ceremony and doctrine, we find, in this cause of charity, justice, and common sense, Mr. Venn, the venerable champion of the Evangelical school, on the same side with Mr. Perry, the indefatigable champion of the Ritualists, and both with the most learned and critical of our Prelates—the Bishop of St. David's. Nor is it a question between Oxford and Cambridge, or between the academical and the practical sections

---

[1] The concurrence of the Archbishop of York with the Archbishop of Canterbury appears from his Charge recently published.

of the Church. The two Universities each speak through the mouths of their Chief Professors of Divinity, and both agree with the long-tried pastoral experience of the Bishop of Carlisle and Mr. Humphry.

On many other points the natural divergences of opinion within the Church, as reflected in the Commission, have prevented a common conclusion which might serve as a basis for action. But on this point the union between otherwise discordant opinions is so strong and so general, as to make the decision one of the most important at which the Commissioners have arrived.

In conclusion, the question which Dean Prideaux addressed to the Convocation of his day may with still greater weight be addressed to our ecclesiastical rulers now—'*And must we always be necessitated 'to pronounce all damned that do not believe every tittle 'in Athanasius' Creed, which so few do understand?*'

It can hardly be doubted that, with all the advantages which this Creed may possess, it has been a burden and a scandal far beyond any use which even its most devoted admirers can claim for it. Without going back to the earlier days of Chillingworth and Baxter, when the conscience of the English Church and nation was first roused against it, there is hardly a young man who has entered Holy Orders in these later days that has not at some time or other been exercised concerning its public use. It is certain that many of its most ardent defenders have as little belief in its condemning clauses as its most serious opponents. However much they may apply them to this or that obnoxious individual, they have ceased to apply them generally. No English clergyman will apply them to the Greek Church or to the American; some even refuse to call them 'damnatory;' some call them 'warning clauses;' some even go so far as to call them 'salvation' clauses. No Nonconformists, whether English or Scottish, Trinitarian or Unitarian, Presbyterian or Independent, have one word of encouragement for it.

There is, therefore, no single school in which a relaxation of its use could fairly be regarded as a grievance. All are alike pledged to allay the scandal which all feel, though they may differ as to the means of removing it. All alike deny its obvious meaning. None wish to retain its general use, except under interpretations far more strained than they apply to any other part of public worship. The objection to it may have assumed an exaggerated importance in the minds of some, but it certainly has, for many years, been, of all the stumbling-blocks in the services of the English Church, the first and foremost.

In the long struggle to remedy this now universally acknowledged evil, sometimes silent, sometimes open, we cannot forbear to select two names, partly to render them due honour, partly because, by reason of their very simplicity, and, so to speak, obscurity, they

H

may stand for many more. One, of whom we will only say a few words, because he is still alive, is that of a venerable layman, now between his eightieth and ninetieth year, the gallant, chivalrous friend of Arnold, whose letters to him outnumber those contained in the correspondence of any other one of his most intimate friends. Few perhaps have read, fewer still now read, the long series of pamphlets of Mr. W. Winstanley Hull, on the Disuse of the Athanasian Creed, remarkable equally for their studied moderation of tone, and for their determined seriousness of purpose. But the persevering efforts which he has waged are a proof of the depth of the feeling which this early scruple engendered. It was the remark of a devout and earnest pastor, long ago called to his reward, when once discussing the Athanasian Creed, 'Whatever ' good it may have done can hardly equal the evil it ' has inflicted on the Church by having kept Mr. Hull ' out of its ministry.'

The other name is that of one who has recently passed away, and whose case deserves a more than passing notice, because it may bring home the difficulties of the subject more fully than any mere general statement.[1]

There are some characters which, without having exercised any commanding influence, or filled any conspicuous position, yet recall to those who knew them a whole world of sacred recollections, and leave behind them a lesson as distinctly and permanently cut in the marble of the memory as any that ever was carved by soldier's sword or poet's pen.

[1] Abridged from the *Norwich Mercury* of March 26, 1870.

CONCLUSION.

Many still live who retain a fond remembrance of that low, picturesque, irregular, prebendal house that once nestled under the west end of Norwich Cathedral, now totally swept out of existence, in which dwelt the gentle genial spirit who for years was the soul of the Norwich Close. One honoured member of that old extinct community still remains— the venerable Professor Sedgwick, whose youthful fire burns unquenched beneath the burden of his octogenarian labours. He, at the time of which we speak, came but as a flashing meteor to and fro, enlightening, cheering, harmonizing all around him, and then retiring from the cloisters, which he made so happy, to the yet more congenial shades of his beloved Cambridge. But he will remember, as will others now long dissevered from East Anglia, how, in all these comings and goings, there always was to be found a steady friend and neighbour in that monastic corner, ever ready with the best advice, with the liveliest sympathy, with the kindliest offer of assistance, with the most opportune suggestion of new occasions for usefulness. This was Charles Wodehouse, who held for many years a canonry of Norwich, and the livings first of Morningthorpe and then of St. Margaret's at Lynn, after which he retired into private life, and on March 17, 1870, in his 80th year, died at Lowestoft.

(1.) Our experience has brought us into contact with many clergymen more able, more learned, more active, than Mr. Wodehouse; but we can truly say that we have rarely known one, who, without brilliant or powerful qualities, more completely represented the best characteristic type of an English clergyman. He was, first, a thorough gentleman, inside and outside to the heart's core, and to the fingers' ends, combining much of the old-fashioned courtesy of other days, with the easier, freer movement of our own time. With this was united a deep, tranquil, religious fervour, coloured visibly, though not exclusively, by the Evangelical revival of his earlier days at Cambridge, not uninfluenced by the burning zeal of the great Quaker family, whose chief pontiff—Joseph John Gurney—resided close to Norwich, and with whom Mr. Wodehouse lived on terms of affectionate intimacy. But beyond this he possessed, in an eminent degree, that firm hold on the old principles of English Church and State which gave to all his teachings and his actions a manly, upright tone; peculiarly grateful to English tastes and English hearts, and which kept alive in him the ennobling, invigorating, humanizing consciousness at once of the citizen of a free country, and of a large-minded Protestant Christian. These are characteristics on which we dwell with more emphasis, because they have of late years become rare. But in his case they gave to his whole manner, doctrine, and conversation a peculiar flavour, which none could mistake, through which his week-days and his Sundays, his politics and his religion, were

Bound each to each by natural piety.

It is remarkable to see, on glancing over the list of his published sermons and pamphlets, how large a proportion bore on questions of social and national concern : how, for example, he turned the subject of the execution of any well-known criminal into an occasion for considering the seriousness of those moments when society is called to vindicate the laws of God and man against their transgressors ; and to consider how far it is itself responsible for the misdeeds of those whom it condemns ; and how fearlessly he delivered his protests against the party spirit and corruption which, even more than in other parts of England, disgraced the elections in the capital of East Anglia—protests which, we may trust, have not been altogether delivered in vain.

Other sermons might be quoted, containing, in the simplest and most unpretending language, enlarged views of the relations of the Church to the Nonconformists in the great common work given to both—of purifying and elevating the masses of their countrymen. His political sympathies, instead of being narrowed by his Churchmanship, were enlarged by it. 'The fact is,' he used to say, 'it 'is impossible to read the New Testament and not per- 'ceive that whatever Christianity has since become, it was 'in its first start a large liberal scheme for the good of the 'world, comprehending all that it could possibly touch, and 'asking the help of all who could possibly co-operate with it.'

(2.) It may be inferred from what has been said, that if ever there was a clergyman who could have pursued at ease the blameless, even tenor of his way, beloved as he was alike by the higher and humbler classes, it was Charles Wodehouse. It is this which gives so instructive, we may almost say, so tragical an interest to the other side of his ministerial career, to which we now turn.

Soon after his promotion to his Norwich canonry, which took place while he was very young, he was forcibly struck by the stringency of the forms then in use for a clergyman's subscription to the Articles and Formularies of the Church of England. Three points in particular seemed to him especially indefensible—the Form of Absolution in the Visitation Service, the Address to Priests in the Ordination Service, and above all, the damnatory clauses of the Athanasian Creed. The more he studied these passages, the more he became convinced, not only of their unsoundness if taken in their obvious and literal sense, but of their unwarrantable intrusion into the Liturgy—the two first not having been introduced into the Church before the thirteenth century, and the last being the work of an unknown author, and condemned by many of the most eminent divines of the English Church. From a very early period in his clerical life he set himself to obtain some redress of this grievance. Pamphlet after pamphlet was published by him on the topic of

Subscription; interview after interview took place with eminent prelates, asking for an authorized sanction of his deviation from the literal sense of these passages. Petition after petition was laid before the House of Lords entreating for the relaxation of the burden of the obligation either of subscription or of use. To these appeals the bishops, though sometimes expressing kindly sympathy, for the most part lent a deaf ear. They refused to stir in the matter themselves. When the matter was stirred by others, they did their best to suppress the movement. One prelate there was—happily for Mr. Wodehouse his own diocesan—who threw himself with ardour into his cause, and steadily supported him in his trying position. The Bishop well knew the value of Mr. Wodehouse as a man and a clergyman, and he was determined not to see him sacrificed for the holding of opinions which he well knew were consciously or unconsciously held by hundreds of clergymen, who had not the clearness of head or of conscience to acknowledge them. On one occasion, on the Bishop's appointment of Mr. Wodehouse to some post of ecclesiastical importance, forty or more clergy remonstrated against the nomination, on the ground of the objections which he had expressed to the Athanasian anathemas. The course which the Bishop took is worth recording. He refused to receive their memorial, unless each one of them separately stated the sense in which *they* accepted the questionable passages. They retired; and it need hardly be said that the memorial was no more heard of. But the protection of a single bishop was not adequate for the permanent retention of the sensitive canon. The scruple which had thus taken possession of a perhaps too susceptible mind, and of which the rulers of the Church at large took so little heed, recurred again and again. He used to say to a friend, 'My dear ———, I have ' no genius—I have no scholarship—to fight this battle. I 'have only one weapon, and that is the resignation of my 'preferment.' That weapon his diocesan would never allow him to use.

Others succeeded, as kindly perhaps disposed towards him, but with a less keen appreciation of his difficulties; and after a struggle of nearly forty years, he ultimately resigned his ecclesiastical position and preferment, and with it the home and sphere in which else he might have lived and died, useful to all around him, and beloved and honoured to the end.

It is painful to think that only within a few years after his retirement into privacy and obscurity—but too late for him to profit by it—an Act was passed by the almost unanimous assent of Parliament and Convocation, abolishing the very form of Subscription that had so oppressed his sensitive mind, and which for so many years so large a portion of the Episcopate and the clergy had refused to touch, or even approach. It is not too much to hope that the same fate awaits the enforced recital of those anathemas, of which he so long pointed out in vain the vexatious burdensomeness, and that the day is near at hand when they will be no more heard in our churches, making sad the hearts of those whom God has not made sad, and strengthening the hands of those whose strength is weakness.

The particular mode in which Mr. Wodehouse worked towards his end may be questioned, but it must have been a satisfaction to him to see that it had not been altogether fruitless. Meanwhile his life remains as a warning to those in the high places of the Church, who having it in their power to retain in its service its best and ablest ministers, either refuse to use that power or defer to use it till it is too late. His life continues also an example to those who remain, not merely in those gentle, persuasive, Christian graces which won their way to every heart, but as a stimulus to all who feel, with him, that the strength of the English Church lies not in its contraction, but in its enlargement; not in imposing burdens, but in removing them. To some, as to him, retirement from a post of honour and duty may seem the best or only weapon that they can use; to others, such retirement may seem to be a step only to be adopted in the very last resort—when the Institution to which we belong has become evidently and hopelessly irreconcileable with the wants of the age. But to all who desire the reform, and hope for the preservation of that Institution, the unceasing struggles of the venerable pastor who now lies in the churchyard of Lowestoft may well be recorded as honourable and edifying incentives in the cause of truth, charity, and honesty, which is the cause of true religion.

It is sometimes said that scruples of individuals cannot be taken into account in large societies, and that individual protests are of no avail against a powerful majority. In the present case it is not without importance to observe that the scruples of individuals have come to represent the feeling of the nation, and that the small minority has become an overwhelming majority. The Creed itself may be long retained as a singular and interesting monument of feelings long gone by. It will still remain in the Prayer-book and Articles of the Church of England as the Solemn League and Covenant remains in the volume of the Standards of the Church of Scotland. Theologians can still have recourse to it as a repertory of arguments, or as an historical statement of belief. Every care should be taken not rudely to shock the associations of those who cling to it as a venerable relic of former times, and who believe it to be a bulwark of doctrines, dear to Christian hearts. The great Biblical truths which the Athanasian Creed enshrines are not dependent on it for their acceptance. It is recorded by a famous mystic, himself a fervent admirer of the Creed, that in his visions of the other world he 'conversed with Athanasius, who said that he could ' find neither the Father, Son, nor Holy Ghost, and ' bitterly complained of his inability.' What is there described in a figure has doubtless been the case with many to whom the logical forms of this Creed have been rather a hindrance than a help towards apprehending the doctrine which it is intended to announce. To those, on the other hand, who find it a stay and a guide, it will not be the less available if it is no longer uttered by unwilling lips to unwilling ears. But the admissions of its defenders have inflicted on its general authority and on its enforced public use a blow which it can never recover; and the large majority of churchmen will rejoice in a relief from a burden which neither Jeremy Taylor nor Tillotson, Chillingworth nor Baxter, were able to bear; whilst all may repose in the wise and holy words of Bishop Ken:—

>Of all the truths that from Thee shine,
>Lord, Thy philanthropy divine
>   Next to my heart still lies,
>   And turns my spiritual eyes
>From all ill-natured schemes design'd
>To bound what Thou hast to no bounds confin'd.

THEOLOGICAL WORKS.

BY BROOKE FOSS WESTCOTT, D.D., Regius
Professor of Divinity in the University of Cambridge.

A GENERAL SURVEY of the HISTORY of the CANON of the NEW TESTAMENT. Third Edition. Crown 8vo. 10s. 6d.

GENERAL VIEW of the HISTORY of the ENGLISH BIBLE. Crown 8vo. 10s. 6d.

INTRODUCTION to the STUDY of the FOUR GOSPELS. Third Edition. Crown 8vo. 10s. 6d.

BY J. B. LIGHTFOOT, D.D., Hulsean Professor of Divinity in the University of Cambridge.

ST. PAUL'S EPISTLE to the GALATIANS. A Revised Text, with Introduction, Notes, and Dissertations. Third Edition. 8vo. 12s.

ST. PAUL'S EPISTLE to the PHILIPPIANS. A Revised Text, with Introduction, Notes, and Dissertations. Second Edition. 8vo. 12s.

S. CLEMENT of ROME. The Two Epistles to the Corinthians. A Revised Text, with Introduction and Notes. 8vo. 8s. 6d.

BY R. CHENEVIX TRENCH, D.D., Archbishop of Dublin.

NOTES on the PARABLES of OUR LORD. Eleventh Edition. 8vo. 12s.

NOTES on the MIRACLES of OUR LORD. Ninth Edition. 8vo. 12s.

STUDIES in the GOSPELS. Second Edition. 8vo. 10s. 6d.

ON the AUTHORISED VERSION of the NEW TESTAMENT. Second Edition. 8vo. 7s.

MACMILLAN & CO., London.

THEOLOGICAL WORKS.

BY DR. VAUGHAN, Master of the Temple.

DISCOURSES on SUBJECTS connected with the LITURGY and WORSHIP of the CHURCH of ENGLAND. Extra fcp. 8vo. 6s.

LECTURES on the REVELATION of ST. JOHN. Third and Cheaper Edition. 2 vols. extra fcp. 8vo. 9s.

ST. PAUL'S EPISTLE to the ROMANS. The Greek Text, with English Notes. Third Edition, much enlarged. Crown 8vo. 7s. 6d.

BY THE REV. CANON KINGSLEY.

GOOD NEWS of GOD. Fourth Edition. Fcp. 8vo. 4s. 6d.

The GOSPEL of the PENTATEUCH. Second Edition. Fcp. 8vo. 4s. 6d.

DISCIPLINE, and other Sermons. Fcp. 8vo. 6s.

VILLAGE SERMONS. Seventh Edition. Fcp. 8vo. 2s. 6d.

BY THE REV. F. D. MAURICE, Professor of Moral Philosophy in the University of Cambridge.

LECTURES on ECCLESIASTICAL HISTORY. 8vo. 10s. 6d.

The RELIGIONS of the WORLD and their RELATIONS to CHRISTIANITY. Fourth Edition. Fcp. 8vo. 5s.

LECTURES on the APOCALYPSE. Crown 8vo. 10s. 6d.

ECCE HOMO. A Survey of the Life and Work of Jesus Christ. Tenth Edition. Crown 8vo. 6s.

The BOOK of ISAIAH CHRONOLOGICALLY ARRANGED. With Historical and Critical Introduction and Explanatory Notes. By T. K. CHEYNE, M.A., Fellow of Balliol College, Oxford. Crown 8vo. 7s. 6d.

The PSALMS CHRONOLOGICALLY ARRANGED. An Amended Version, with Historical Introductions and Explanatory Notes. By FOUR FRIENDS. Second and Cheaper Edition. Crown 8vo. 8s. 6d. (STUDENTS' EDITION, with briefer Notes, 18mo. 3s. 6d.)

MACMILLAN & CO., London.

www.ingramcontent.com/pod-product-compliance
Lightning Source LLC
Chambersburg PA
CBHW020122170426
43199CB00009B/600